THE LIFE OF BRI II

THE SWINGING 60's

BY

BRIAN HAMBLETT

COVER DESIGN BY MAX HAMBLETT

1

For my mother, the rock on which this writer was built.

CONTENT

FOREWORD

By Stewart Neale (my co-star in my books)

I can't speak from personal experience, but it does seem that 1990 heralded the end of the 'magical childhood!' It was about that time that I noticed the lack of children playing out in the streets of Moston, Manchester, where Brian and myself grew up and came of age. Those I did notice just skulked around under their hoodies sat on a BMX ... usually stolen.

There was no sign of the kids who couldn't find a ball to play with so used a tin can ... no kids using a purloined broomstick handle that had been sharpened to point as a spear ... no kids in grey shorts and socks threatening to disappear into their shoes with a homemade catapult hanging casually from a back pocket. It was as if a whole breed of child had become extinct!

Home computers and games consoles are indeed wondrous things, but their introduction seems to have sounded the death knell in a very short period of time of an 'innocent childhood'. No more would we see kids using a branch from a tree as a Winchester rifle whilst playing 'cowboys and injuns ... or as it is known nowadays ... 'cowpersons and first Nations'! These days that stick would not be able to double as a machine gun for shooting the 'Jerries' (or in my case the damn 'Tommies') with, if it was used at all it would be a laser target designator for locking laser guided missiles ... better the Tommy gun, there is not 'rat a tat...rat a tat' sound effect with a laser!

No more do we see ramshackle 'guiders' (or bogies or go-karts whichever your preference) thrown together lovingly from old pram wheels, planks of wood and an orange crate stolen from the Greengrocers! No, kids these days choose to ride about in motorised mini replicas of BMW's, Ferrari's and the odd Rolls Royce. We would search for miles looking for discarded bicycles, which we would then cannibalise and rebuild into our own personal 'tracker' bikes, complete with cow horn handle bars.

Truly the 90's brought the end of a golden period of childhood ... but then that's only the opinion of a 'grumpy old fogey'!

If you hanker after those days of idyllic, long summers of laughter ... if you yearn to dip in to the nostalgia of that 'time gone by', halcyon days of deprived, but joyous, pre-pubescent juveniles ... hopefully the stories held within this book will go some way to bring back some of that magic ... read on and I'm confident that adventures, scrapes and predicaments Brian and myself got into came give you a few chuckles along the way and maybe the odd tear.

We all have our own personal childhood memories, but as we trundle along this weary road of life to its inevitable conclusion we can tend to sideline and forget about them stress free days ... if you were a child between 1950-1990 then much of what you are about to read may, hopefully, transport you back and bring a smile to your face.

Stewart Neale
Sweden 2014

DRESSED TO KILL

"Are you sure?" mum asked as she stepped back for a better look at my appearance.

"Yes, no one else will go as him." I said confidently.

"Nope, I am absolutely sure you will be the only one. Do you want a name badge? To be honest it's not instantly obvious who you are supposed to be."

"Did you ever see him wear a name badge?" I asked.

"No, but he usually wore a suit, and you haven't got one of them on, either.

"But I have got a white shirt and black tie just like the ones he wore." I smiled and opened my arms in a 'voila' motion.

"I'm still not convinced people will know who you are."

There came a knock at the front door. Mum walked towards it, glancing back at me with tightly scrunched up eyes, and then shaking her head. She opened the door and then focused on the image in front of her.

"Oh, Stewart dear, you look, erm very, what's the word? Teutonic?"

"Thanks, Marie, that's the look I was going for. I'm Adolf Hitler!" he clicked his heels and raised his right arm in the Nazi salute. "Heil Marie. Har har, is Bri ready?"

"I think so. Brian, the leader of the 1000 year Reich is here for you."

"Right, coming." I walked out of the kitchen stabbing my feet into my shoes, whose laces had not been untied from their previous wearing.

"Hey, Stew, wow that's great. You look like a dwarf Hitler."

"Who are you supposed to be?" his face had confusion etched all over it.

"I'm Martin Luther King!" I smiled, my white teeth shone like polished opals out of my boot polished face.

"Who?"

"Martin Luther King, the civil rights leader who was shot last year." I explained. "Mum, we're off to school now, see 'ya lator'." I grabbed a plastic bag and departed. She followed us to the street corner and watched us as we ambled up Rudd Street towards the Diggy. Chatting and laughing as we headed to school. From the back she could see my white legs and hands and even the ebony colour of the back of my ears.

She grimaced at the memory of putting Cherry Blossom boot polish on my face, but glad she had refused to do the legs. It would take long enough getting my face back to something resembling flesh tones.

This was the first time Lily Lane School had held a fancy dress day. We had to donate sixpence to the school fund and we could come dressed as our heroes.

"Morning, morning, morn … good God!" Mr. Beckett was welcoming the children as they entered the school by the Lizmar Terrace entrance.

"Morning Sir." we said in unison.

"Adolf Hitler!" he exclaimed. "This is supposed to be a day of heroes."

"Well … he wrote a book, invented the Volkswagen Beetle and got the Autobahn built, sir!" Stew claimed.

"What about his war crimes?" he asked rhetorically.

"Well I've been reading a book, and apparently the Allies may have made most of it up." Stew answered anyway. "...conspiracy, sir."

"What, the Second World War was all made up? My father fought against Germany! Or did he just pretend to be fighting for six years? Was he sunning himself on the French Riviera??"

"No, not that bit. Just the bad bits, you know, Belsen and things. The rest was just a fair fight."

"Neale, you never fail to leave me lost for words. I despair for your future." he turned to me and did a double take. "What on Earth are you, Hamblett?"

"Sir, I'm… "

"He's Louis Armstrong, sir."

"Oh, very good. Have you padded your stomach? You look chubbier, very good, I like a bit of Satchmo myself." he patted my head.

"No sir, I'm… hey! I haven't padded my belly!" but he moved me along and greeted another Armstrong, a moon walking one with a large plastic, see through, bowl over his head as a helmet.

"Look at you, one small step for a boy, one... oooh, can you breath in there?" he asked as Stephen Miller started to sway drunkenly in front of him. "... Take it off boy. There's no air holes is there?" he pulled at the 'helmet', which was sellotaped to his neck. It was hard to tell if he was suffocating in the helmet or had strangulated himself wrapping the sellotape round his neck. Seconds later Miller was gulping fresh air back into his lungs.

We walked into the yard, surrounded by three Elvis Presley's and a Georgie Best, There was a few Twiggy's and an even one Raquel Welch. That wasn't as sexy as it sounds, although he looked very convincing, Fred Hewitt was no Raquel Welch!

"Hello Stewart." said Mr. Roney as he roamed the yard, keeping order.

"Seig Heil, Herr Klassenlehrer!" the hell click and swift lifting of his arm in salute.

"Brian?" he looked at me and studied me.

"I'm... "I started.

"He's a blackhead sir. Squeeze him, he spits custard out of his mouth."

"Oh, not really a hero ... but very original."

"No sir, I've come as..." but he had moved away to a small group of John Wayne's. "Stop telling everyone I'm something stupid." I railed at the toothbrush moustachioed Nazi.

"Oh, don't be soft, it's just a laugh."

"Well, it's me that everyone is laughing at."

12

"Well, just painting your head black ain't very good, is it? Look at John Loftus, now he's made an effort, he's like a dehydrated Eamonn Andrews! All suited up and stood there with his big red book saying to anybody who'd listen… 'Thus is yuuur loife'."

"I just thought a man who had given all them black people hope of being equal to the white people in America was someone special."

"He must have been special or the Yanks wouldn't have shot him, would they? But you've just painted your head black, you look like a dead match!"

"Line up everybody, time to go in." the teacher called. Stew joined his classmates of Superheroes, footballers and pop stars while I filed into the school with my year.

****

The morning assembly had included hymns and a small reading from our headmaster Mr. Beckett, a small man who had the fastest growing bristles in Western Europe, he entered the school in the morning clean shaven and by lunch he was able to plait corn rows in his beard!

"Each and every one of you look wonderful." he stroked his arm across in front of him indicating to the seated cross legged children. "Now I've been told that each class has voted for their favourite character and they are going to join me on stage now." he was handed a piece of paper by one of the teachers sat behind him. "

"From the First year we have Tommy Duckworth…" he looked at the first two rows sat immediately in front of him. A child stood, he was

13

dressed as Superman. "Here, boy." Beckett indicated for the boy to join him. He sidestepped his peers and walked up the three steps at the side of the stage and stood by the headmaster, head bowed shyly.

"Now, Thomas, explain to everybody why Superman is your hero."

"Superman is my hero 'cos he can fly." he whispered.

"Louder, son. Is it because he fights evil?" he smiled.

"Who's Ethel?" Tommy asked bemused, looking around.

"Not Ethel, evil … you know, the baddies." Beckett smiled uncomfortably.

"No, I like 'im 'cos he flies!" Tommy insisted.

"Okay, let's give Thomas a big hand." the headmaster began clapping and urged the throng of assembled pupils to join in.

"Next, from year two, is Alison Braithwaite…" he read out and then peered out for some movement.

A girl stood, dressed as a nurse and carrying a lantern. She was a whole year older than the previous winner, who stood, hopping from one foot to the next impatiently in his cape by the back curtains.

"Up you come Alison, I know who you are." he smiled at her.

"I know who you are, too." she replied. "You're Mr. Biscuit."

"Beckett, child, Mr. Beck … ett!" he shook his head, as the children giggled at her mistake. He thought, had they all voted for the village idiots out of pity?

"Sirry sor … I mean sorry sir." she walked to his side and turned and faced the audience. "Hello…" she did a little wave to her friends.

"Are you Florence Nightingale, Alison? Speak up so everyone can hear you." He whispered to her bending down to her height, both hands on his knees.

"No, I'm the 'lady of the night'!" she shouted at the top of her voice.

Beckett gasped at her statement. Only Stewart understood her mistake and so laughed alone amongst the assembled children. Stew was already more advanced in that department than any other child there … and some of the teachers too! The teachers that stood along the wall coughed and tried to hide their amusement.

"You mean the Lady of the Lamp, Alison … Lady of the Lamp. Wonderful. She wandered the hospital tents during the Crimean War, bringing hope to the infirm. A real heroine." he explained to everybody, his face taking on a crimson hue.

"Thank you Alison, join Thomas at the back. Next, year … erm, three, I think." he pulled the paper from his jacket pocket and perused the list. "Yes, year three, and it is … Brian Hamblett?" he didn't even try to hide his disappointment, he had a deep hatred of me because I refused to stop talking in class.

I leapt to my feet and made my way to the side. I hadn't actually won any votes in my class! I was the only child willing to go on stage!

"Hello Sir." I put my white hand out to shake his. He never let go off the paper. The children were all laughing now, some were pointing at my black face.

"Hamblett." he scratched his head in wonderment. "Well done. Today children, Hamblett has come as his hero, the Jazz trumpeter and singer…" I interrupted him.

"Sir, I'm not Lewis Armstrong."

"Louis, not Lewis." he smiled that smarmy smile.

"I'm not 'im either, I'm Martin Luther King." I smiled proudly, the laughing was growing. Someone called out 'more like Martin Luther Queen'!

"This is becoming a farce, Hamblett, you can't chop and change your identity willy nilly." Beckett whispered harshly.

"I haven't, I've always been Martin Luther King."

"You told me … oh … it doesn't matter now." he turned and addressed the audience again. "My mistake, apparently Hamblett, the human chameleon is now Martin Luther King." he breathed out heavily then composed himself.

"Martin Luther King, very good." he clapped and indicated for me to join the two at the back of the stage.

"Sir, I learnt something to say." I grinned at him.

"Hey?" he uttered, his hand still pointing to the back.

"I learnt something to say. 'Bout Mr. King."

"Oh, alright." his hand swept forward from the curtains to the boys and girls assembled. "Be quick,

16

please." he said under his breath. He stood back and crossed his arms in annoyance.

I walked to the side of the grey suited headmaster and stood at the lectern and unfolded a small piece of paper, this unfolding went on… and on… and on. Beckett gave a large cough, I turned and smiled showing him the finally unfolded sheet. I turned and faced the crowd.

"I have a dream … let freedom ring from Stone Mountain of Georgia.

Let freedom ring from Lookout Mountain of Tennessee.

Let freedom ring out from every hill and molehill of Mississippi.

From every mountainside, let freedom ring." my voice was rising with each sentence.

And when this happens, and when we allow freedom ring, when we it ring from every village and every hamlet, from every state and every city, we will be able to speed up that day when all…" I put large emphasise on the word all. "… of God's children, black men and white men, Jews and gentiles, Protestants and Catholics, will be able to join hands and sing in the words of the old Negro song…

Free at last! Thank God almighty, we are free at last!" I stopped and there was silence. I began the slow process of folding back up my speech again when Mr. Roney began clapping to my right. Then more and more hands came together and a cheer went up. I looked up from my folding and looked out to the audience, then looked around at the face of Mr. Beckett. His lantern jaw was tight, his eyes cold. I grinned my Stan Laurel smile at him, he finally accepted I had done something right … at last … and he finally joined in the applause. As he clapped his shirt sleeves rode up slightly revealing bunches of dark, coarse hair on his forearms. He had a similar sprouting at his Adams apple, it looked like black coconut fur.

I thought to myself, my headmaster is probably half chimpanzee when he's naked, as the applause faded I was still imagining him hanging from the monkey ropes that were our school 'gym', in my mind's eye he had a half peeled banana in hand and chattering wildly to himself.

"Hamblett, Hamblett." I was roused from my reverie by a hand shaking my shoulder. "Hamblett, well done, but join the other two at the back, now." I smiled broadly at my 'Planet of the Apes' headmaster and wandered happily to the back.

"Now." he started again. "The last pupil to come up will be…." he unfolded the paper again and stopped dead. He stared at teachers assembled against the wall, they were all checking their shoes. He turned to the deputy headmaster sat on the stage and ushered him forward. There was a small 'conflab', some head shaking and nodding from both, then he turned to the kids again. "… Stewart Neale!" he stuttered.

A small, single cheer went up at the back where the oldest children were sat, and from exactly where the cheer originated, Stewart stood. Gleaming from ear to ear and punching the air, he strode, stepping on all his classmates indiscriminately. He jogged up the aisle where the teachers stood, his hand high for a high five … he got a high nothing! Unmoved he hopped up onto the stage. He had, admittedly, removed the Hitler 'tasche and the Iron Cross from his chest. The Swastika armband was nowhere to be seen so it was a relieved Mr. Beckett that received the uniformed child reluctantly.

"Hello Sir." Stewart said happily. He turned and gave me the thumbs up and a 'can you believe it' face.

"Hello Neale." he said quietly and added. "I've been told you have changed to Lord Baden Powell, though I'm not sure he wore wellington boots like those." he pointed down at Stews feeble attempt at SS jackboots.

"Bet he wore 'em when it was raining, sir, especially when he was camping out. I went camping once and it got that muddy I had to pee…"

"Neale." he interrupted. "Just turn and explain, and briefly mind, why Baden Powell is your hero. Leave your toilet habits in you lurid mind, please" he pushed Stew towards the lectern.

"Hello everybody," He waved to all the school. "I've come today as Robert Robertson Smyth Baden-Powell, he started the Scouts for boys a dead long time ago. I bet Mr. Beckett remembers because he's old, aren't you sir?" he looked at the reddening face of our head. "Powell was in the army and he helped batter the South Africans in the Boring War. I think it was him that started Concentration camps, Adolf Hitler got all the blame for doing it but no one ever moans at Baden Pow…owwww." Stewart squealed as he was grabbed by the shoulders and walked quickly to the rear curtain where he stood next to me. The teacher took her hands off him and looked at him with disgust before wandering back to the side.

"You had to get Adolf in there, didn't you?" I whispered.

"Just telling it as it is, Hammy. It's the same old story, the winning army get to write the history books."

"I still think you may be a little too right wing for an eleven year old."

"Nah, I'm just playing mind games with everyone. Although ..." he put his mouth nearer to my ear and said in even more hushed tones. " ...did you see that speech by another Powell last night, Enoch Powell, that's it? Rivers of blood, that's what he said, rivers of blood. Now he seems like someone I could look up to ... he'll make a mighty fine Prime Minister!"

RACIAL HARMONY

I'd burst through the front door, failing to close it behind me.

"Was you born in a barn?" mum asked sarcastically.

"You should know, you was there, weren't you? He he."

"Less of the lip young man. What are you doing in the kitchen?"

"Making a jam butty."

"Tidy up after yourself, please." she asked forlornly.

"Awww mum, can you? I'm playing out."

"I suppose so, but don't leave jam on the table, floor, and knife and in the butter."

"Ermmm," the request may have come a little late.

"What are you playing?" she asked as she entered the kitchen.

"Oh," I turned and looked at her. "We're just running away from the Black kids." I smiled.

"You're what?" her voice nearly broke the kitchen window.

"We don't want to play with the Blackie's so we keep hiding from them."

"Brian Hamblett Junior!" she put her hands on her hips, a Universal sign of outrage and anger in the mothers 'union'.

"What?" I asked then took a bite of thick white crust of bread lathered in real butter and strawberry jam, "I don't want to catch something off 'em!"

"I am disgusted! I have not brought you up to be like that. Are they upset?"

"Yeah, a bit, but…"

"No buts, I am disappointed in you."

"For what? I don't want to get the dreaded 'lurgy'!"

"Give me that." she yanked the bread out of my hand. "Go upstairs and think about what you are doing, go on." she pointed to the ceiling, approximately where my bedroom was waiting.

"Mum, it's not just me, Stewart is running away from them too, and Digger and Geoff. No one wants to play with 'em."

"Those poor children, all they want to do is play with you. We are all the same under the skin, son. Go to your room."

"I never said they had different 'skellingtons'!"

"If you think this is the time for 'sarky' comments like that … well sunny Jim, you are way out of line!"

"I don't know what I've done wrong!"

"Go … I'll send your father up to talk to you about racism … then maybe you'll understand!" she took a breath, "It won't help that he doesn't like the Egyptians or the Japanese, and he's not keen on the French or Italians … but that's more to do with the war. He can talk some sense into you."

Half an hour later I heard my dad's whistle coming down Lakin Street … happy and tuneful, happy with the World. There was the metallic scratching of a key in the lock then the front door banged shut. There was a mumbling of chatter through the ceiling as I heard my mother telling him of my behavior.

Dad took the stairs two at a time and opened my door.

"Okay, what's all this about?" he had a frown on his face, this was a rare feature. I sat on my bed and explained my behavior.

Five minutes later I was led into the living room, dad had his hand on my shoulder. I hung my head so I didn't have to make eye contact with my mother.

"Have you told him?" she asked my dad.

"I've spoken to him." he admitted.

"Does he understand this is not acceptable behavior? Skin colour isn't important?" she said passionately.

"Well I started to but I think this may be a big misunderstanding. Explain Bri."

I looked up at my confused mother and waited for her to look down from my dad.

"We were running away from the Blackie's…"

"Please don't say that, it's a horrible way to talk about coloured children."

"Rickie and Janice Black aren't coloured mum! They are white and we are running away from them 'cos they've got chicken pox!"

"It's their nickname, Nod. Blackie, short for…"

"Yes, I know how a nickname works, Brian!" she cut dad short.

"I don't think they should be playing out with all them spots, do you, mum?"

"No, probably not." she turned and walked to the sink.

"Can I play out now?"

"Yes, go on. Next time explain yourself better."

"Where's me jam butty?" I asked as I scanned all the kitchen surfaces.

"Oh, I put it in the bin. I'm sorry."

"It's alright, I've got it."

"Don't eat food out of the bin." she made a lunge towards me, but I was already through to the front door.

"It's fine, just got a bit of chicken skin on it from last night's tea … and I like chicken skin! See you later."

"You are disgusting, I never brought you up to do that … and you," she said to my dad "Don't you say a word about any of what's happened today … understand?" a hint of venom were in her words as she passed my father on her way back to the sink.

"As if I would." his grin was broad and sincere. "As if I would!"

THREE DUMMIES

"Mum, it's not here, I've looked everywhere and it's not even under my bed!" the desperation was tangible in my squealing voice.

"Well son, where did you have it last, I certainly haven't been using him, I can't bear the sight of him, he gives me the willy's to be honest." her voice got louder as she exited her bedroom and popped her head into mine. "Oh, and I hope you are putting everything back where it came from, look at the mess, you scruffy ha'porth!"

"I'll do it later, I need to find me doll. Why do you have to tidy up all the time?!" I fumed.

"So we don't live in a rubbish tip, now, calm down, it can't be far, son," she had started picking up a battalion of action men and single socks, marbles of different colours and sizes and tiny, green toy soldiers as she tried to calm me.

"But I knew where everything was, then you go and tidy up and I can't find a single thing, it's easier just to leave 'em where they are." I sat back against my bedroom wall, my dark brown eyes looking beyond her and into the past, trying to remember when I had last used Edward Woodhead, my ventriloquist doll, in my mind's eye I could see his big red lips and white wooden teeth grinning at me, but where was he hiding?

"I know it would, but we don't live in a tip. What if 'you' tried tidying up, then you would know where everything was, wouldn't you? Look, try in the cupboard under the stairs, while I try to sort this mess out, my God, you're a one man typhoon!"

"Mum, whatcha talking about? I'm not a typhoon am I? I ain't got no money at all!" this was blurted out as I raced past her, heading for the stairs.

"Typhoon, not a tycoo...oo...oh, what's the point?" she was already talking to a fast, closing door.

I slammed my tiny, sockless feet, as hard as possible into each and every step of the stairs, the wood under the thin carpet reverberated as I bombed downwards. I needed the use of both outstretched arms to stop me crashing into the wall at the bottom, and like a rubber ball I let my arms collapse slightly under my weight, then with a push of my hands I was heading left into the kitchen. There was a space set under the stairs, it was for shoes, coats and the larger items that wouldn't fit in drawers. I pulled the door open and stared into the gloomy void. Nothing obvious, this required illumination.

On the left hand side was a brown, round light switch, in the classic jelly mould shape. I flicked it into the on position, the light was instant and bright, within seconds I was clambering into the ever narrowing space, and the ceiling was falling in time with the stairs above, like a wedge of cheese. The further back I got, the murkier the light became, my body blocking the bulbs 60 watt radiance.

Then, there, at the very back, lay like a victim of a very serious road accident, was Edward. Still smiling, even though he had one foot placed adjacent to his right ear and his head was turned 180 degrees from its natural position. His permanent smile suggested he was overjoyed at the thought of me jamming my hand up his backside again, and having the opportunity to chat again, with that horrendous speech impediment I created for him.

All this searching had been brought about by the opportunity of winning a whole three pounds and a large silver cup in the St. Dunstan's Summer Fair Talent contest, an annual competition for all age groups. I would be entering the under 11's section and I was determined that me and Edward would be walking off with the cup.

With Edward in hand I began my reverse exit, each step was taken stealthily, my feet searching tentatively for solid ground before putting my weight on the slippered foot, eventually using my backside to push the door open and see my dummy in daylight.

"Got him Mum." I screamed loudly.

"I'm only here, love!" it was my mother, just two feet behind me. "And now I'm partially deaf!" she was wiggling fingers in her ears.

"I ain't got eyes in the back of my head though, have I? I said a little too defensively.

"I beg your pardon." Mum stared me down, waiting for an apology.

"Sorry, mum." this time quieter, this time with my head bowed and this time with contrition.

"That's better, I didn't bring you up to be cheeky, now, did I?"

"No Mum, but I can't know where you are all the time, can I?" softer still.

"No, but I really don't think shouting is the best form of communication, you do shout a little bit too often. What's your plans now you've found that wooden monster? She asked, glancing with distaste at my ventriloquist doll.

"Gonna go to Stew's, I'm gonna practice and practice so I'm dead good, and win that cup." my voice had found some depth again, visualising victory.

"Well, it's not the winning, is it son? It's the taking part." she smiled.

"Whatttt!" I started. "Course it's about the winning! Flipping 'eck, what's the point in even doing it if I don't win?" I shook my head in disbelief.

"Oh dear son, now don't be getting upset if you don't win."

"I'm off to Stew's, you're really bringing me down now, not even started and you've got me losing" I turned and slowly walked towards the front door, a ventriloquist doll thrown over my shoulder, each step making his eyes blink, Mum found this incredibly disturbing and she felt a shiver run the length of her spine as the upside down head appeared to wink at her.

"Brian, take Trumper with you, he's not been out today."

"'Okay, Trumps. Come on, boy" the four legged beast with dirty white frizzy hair, looking more like a Rastafarian with each passing year, struggled to his

29

feet from in front of an open fire, his front legs moved way out in front of him and he stretched head down leaving his hind legs rigid and his buttocks in the air, he yawned and his tongue rolled out like a red carpet and then slowly curled back in. He rose completely and followed me to the front door. I opened the door and held it open, he stopped and glanced up at the tiny humanoid body over my right shoulder then continued passed me into the open air.

"See ya later." I shouted.

"Don't shout! Enjoy yourself and don't let Stew put a hangman's noose round Edwards neck again, he's a right destructive, little sod." by the end of the sentence she realised I wasn't there to listen, and to her annoyance, had left the front door wide open.

"How difficult can it be to close a door?" she walked over and closed it shut.

I knocked on Stew's door, it had two steps to the front door, and I had stood back so I wasn't potentially looking into the groin of an adult when the door was answered. I saw through the glass that someone had left the living room and was approaching. The silhouette loomed large and an arm reached up and the door was pulled open.

Stew's Dad stood staring at me, Trumper and Edward.

"Oh, look at this, a dummy...."

"It's my ventriloquist doll..."

"No, I was talking about you! The only one of you three with a brain is that hound" he laughed.

"Er, I don't fink so..." I stuttered, "Is Stewart in?" I knew this was going to be torture, it's easier to just let him have his fun. My friend's fathers really were a nightmare, constantly teasing. I'd decided some time ago, if I had kids when I get really old like them, I'm going to be smashing to all their friends.

"Stewart," he called, "Deirdre's here for you!" He didn't retire to the living room, he just stood stock still thinking up something to irritate.

"It's Brian." I said quietly in a deadpan voice, bending to one side to bypass his father's body.

"Who?" a voice shouted from further down the hallway, out of the living room.

"Deirdre, and she says she loves you." Guy never took his eyes off me, his grin got bigger and bigger at my obvious discomfort.

"It's Brian, and I'm not a girl." I said this louder, hoping Stew would hear me. I kept my head down now so Stew's dad couldn't make eye contact.

"Oh, it's Hammy, come in." Stew's head had popped round the living room door and spotted me.

"In you come, Deirdre ... and bring your smelly friends" another snigger from his Dad as he stood slightly to one side. I entered side on to squeeze past him and Stew opened the door to the front room, I was relieved, it would vacant of adults. Trumper followed us in. It was nice and cool, the room had a large window that looked out onto Lakin Street, brilliant white lace curtains hung down preserving a little privacy.

"Your Dad does my head in." I said with a frown.

"How do you think I feel when I call for you and your Dad puts his slipper on his head while I am sat there, then ten minutes later he tells me you're not even in the house? Dads, they're all mad."

Over the next few hours we garnered together a plan. Edward would be manipulated by me on stage, he would be a memory man. Stew would be a stooge in the audience, and I would pick him to ask any five questions he wanted to test Edwards's general knowledge. He would then ask pre-determined trivia that Edward, with my ventriloquist dexterity, would answer, bringing the audience to their feet. Who couldn't love a ventriloquist doll who also happened to be a memory man?

We used Stew's Amazing Magic Robot to get the questions. This was brilliant game, it had a little metal robot with a long stick, the robot would be placed centrally in the middle of a small circle of questions, and he would spin around quickly then stop with the stick pointing at one of the questions. We would then move the robot to the middle of an adjacent circle, this time it was a selection of answers. Again he would spin around and let his stick settle ... always on the correct answer to the previous question. In between all this, we would both be screaming and shouting out what each of us believed was the right answer ... and the little tin man would decide.

We had chosen the questions and answers that would be used in the contest, I had written them down on two A4 sheets, one for Stew and one for me, we would need to memorise these so as not to end up looking like complete fools.

At tea time, Trumper followed me home, all I had to do now was practice our agreed routine and with luck the money and cup would be ours, and in my head I had already begun spending my share of the spoils.

I reached my house and opened the front door, and shouted out.

"Only me." I walked in to find Mum putting together the Evening News, some was spread over the floor, some sheets were fluttering down "What's happened to the paper?" I asked scanning the floor.

"What do you mean, what's happened to the paper? When somebody bursts in through the front door screaming like a banshee it can make a person throw a paper in the air in flaming shock ... why do you insist on shouting that 'only you,' when you come in through the front door ... I'm going to have a heart attack one of these days!" she said as sternly as she was able, which really didn't come across as stern at all, it was more a mild agitation by the end of the sentence.

"Sorrrrreeee, you'd think you'd be happy it wasn't a thief ... next time I'll say nothing, and then what if I'm a cat burglar, here to burglar...er..ize us, then you'd be sorry, just 'cos you made me be silent we'd have everything pinched..." I emphasised this crazy logic by putting my hands on my hips, while looking down at her, on all fours, trying to re-insert the television page into its correct position. I appeared to have vented for nothing, she just ignored me.

"Trumper, you are not helping by lying on the sports pages." she looked at me. "You, me-laddo, upstairs and get changed, I've tidied your room, do...not...make...a...mess." she said ever so slowly so I would understand.

"Flipping 'eck, I bet even more toys will have gone missing now," I muttered as I turned for the door.

"Thank you, mum." my Mother said sarcastically.

"Oh, is Nana here?" I asked whizzing round.

"Pardon?"

"You said thanks Mum … and your mum's 'me' Nana, isn't she?"

"No….erm, well, yes, but...oh, I was just being sarcastic. You should have just said thank you mum." she struggled to explain herself.

"Oh, okay," I was totally lost now, "Er, thanks Mum!!" I gave her a quizzical look to see if this was right. She nodded ever so slightly.

"Deary, deary me, Brian, it's pointless, isn't it? Just go upstairs!"

"What? What have I done now?" I asked in exasperation.

"Nothing, you never do anything, dear, up the Mollies and get changed into your jammies, you're not going out again tonight."

"What's for tea?" I called from the kitchen.

"Chop, egg and chips."

"Ooooh, lovely, don't cut the fat off me chop, that's me favourite bit.

"Just go and get ready, I'll put it under the grill now."

Once tea had been eaten and the pots washed, I watched Coronation Street with Mum and Trumper. Dad was driving his truck up to Glasgow and staying out overnight and wouldn't be home until tomorrow.

It was still light out but the option of playing out had gone, so when the credits rolled, I decided to go upstairs and do some practice with Edward.

"Come on Trumper, you can be my audience."

Reluctantly he rose and followed, he gave Mum a glance, hoping for a reprieve. None came, Mum was lifting up the Evening News, seconds later it was lowered, her front page was still upside down from the trauma earlier in the day.

I sat on my bed, Trumper lay on the rug below me. I lifted Edward up and sat him on my knee, his legs loose and dangling, I twirled his head a couple of times, and this made Trumper do a double take. Then I settled, I took a breath and clamped my teeth together.

"Herro, radies and gentlemen, my name ish Grian ... oh flipping eck ... I'm supposed to talk normal, aren't I?" I began again, "Hello, ladies and gentlemen, my name is Brian, and my friend here is called Edward, say hello Edward."

"Herro everygoddy, niysh to shee you." Trumper watched intently as Edwards teeth chomped up and down, the voice didn't sync with the lips, it was like the worst dubbing of a foreign film ever.

"Hey Trumper, I've not lost it, have I?" my self-belief so much higher than my talent, and so I ploughed on, mercilessly punishing both Edwards wooden chops and Trumpers sensitive ears.

*

When the morning of the show finally arrived, the weeks of practice had meant I had attained the highest level of ventriloquism I would ever reach, which was still incredibly low! Through a mixture of stoic parental support and my own incredible naivety, my confidence was sky high. Stewart was ready to play the part of the 'stooge' secreted in the watching assembly ... what could go wrong?

I would invite the audience to ask any question to my wooden friend, I expected hands to shoot up all across the crowd, but I would select Stew to interrogate Edward with a selection of trivia ... the multitude would gasp at my ventriloquistic skills and Edwards knowledge of the difficult questions Stew fired at him/me. While I had lay in bed at night, I had imagined them on their feet, applauding, whistling, shouting my name ... and then me, up on stage, accepting the plaudits, prize money and cup.

I awoke to the sun blazing into my room, the window was open slightly and I could hear the harsh calls of magpies as they warned their friends of a prowling cat in the neighbourhood. I had pushed my single white linen sheet off me sometime in the night, and it now covered Trumper, who lay on the bed at my feet, snoring under the sheet, still comatose.

On rising, I slipped my legs on to the floor, let them feel about for their slippers unsuccessfully, while at the same time stretched my arms up towards the ceiling, an enormous yawn escaped my mouth. I stood and passed the bucket at the bottom of my bed, it hadn't been needed in the night so it was urine free.

Mum always put my underpants and socks in the lowest drawer in the large oak chest at the bottom of my bed, a selection of simple grey socks to the left and my undies to the right, these too were all near identical, off white Y fronts.

One drawer up were my tee shirts, a royal blue, bri-nylon one took my eye immediately and I dragged it free but at the same time I managed to pull three others, that had lay on top of it, out at the same time. All my mother's ironing and patient folding was laid to waste in a split second as I pulled it free and bundled the unrequired ones back in firmly, shoving and pushing, unworried by the creasing, until I was able to get the drawer nearly closed and still somehow I managed to leave a sleeve of one of them dangling out.

Once my chosen garments were donned, I dropped to my knees, my bum was sticking in the air, and looked under my bed, in no time I had spotted my grey shorts and black snake belt, both were crumpled in a small heap by an upturned compendium of games box from last Christmas. There was a small dice, a partially deflated black and white football, a selection of Action men and their weaponry, a teaspoon and an empty, dark blue packet of salt from some crisps I had sneaked upstairs a couple of nights ago all scattered around, all hidden out of sight.

"Come on Trumper, let's see what's for breakfast." I walked towards the door, stopped momentarily as I fiddled with my snake belt, making sure it was clipped in place correctly.

I pulled open the door and carefully descended the stairs, one hand on the bannister the other sliding down the wallpaper, behind me I could hear Trumper coming down just as cautiously, you really needed to be fully awake before you dared pick up any real pace on this precipitous staircase.

I reached the bottom step and turned left, there was a wooden door to open before I entered the cool kitchen. Mum was by the sink, sun shining on her through the window in front of her, her hands were in soapy water. She turned and smiled at me.

"Morning handsome." she said brightly.

"Morning mum, what's for breakfast?"

"Toast. Okay?" she asked over her shoulder.

"Great, some Vimto too, please." I replied.

She pulled the plug out of the sink, the slurping and gurgling of escaping water was loud. Mum picked the tea towel up from the drainer and wiped her hands carefully.

"Here, teeth first." she leaned over the sink and picked my toothbrush from the glass on the window sill.

"What? Clean my teeth, then just dirty 'em again with toast? Does that any sense at all?" I asked incredulously.

"You really do overthink things Brian. You clean them after your breakfast if you really want to..." she relented. "...as long as you clean them properly!"

"Deal."

"Is it the talent contest today?" she enquired.

"It is Mum, and me and Edward are gonna win." I said confidently.

She turned from putting bread under the eye level grill, and looked at me.

"Does this mean they'll be no more of those conversations where you talk through gritted teeth?" she gave me a hopeful grin.

"You know why I had to do that, Mum, I needed to test my 'ventriloquising' skills, so I could get dead good!" I explained why all communications over the preceding days had been via Edward, even when Edward wasn't actually with me.

"I know, love, but I'm really glad you are back to talking normal now, I was getting a little worried you get a speech impediment." she smiled as she turned to check on my toast.

"What? Have my teeth jammed together … forever? I wouldn't have been able to eat me toast!" I started. "And, eventually, I could've starved to death!" I looked at mum with wide eyes.

"And what a loss that would of been to the world of ventriloquism, hey?" she exclaimed in mock joy as she buttered my toast.

Mum supplied me with my purple coloured cordial and two slabs of thick white toasted bread, the butter was cut like cheese and it was melting slowly into the golden brown surface. The first bite created a crisp loud crunch that put a smile on both our faces … I ate the rest like someone was about to slit my throat, a bite of toast, a couple of chews then a slosh of Vimto. At my feet, sat on his haunches, staring at me, Trumper. His, grey tail, looking like one of my granddads discarded pipe cleaners, flapped intermittently, his dark brown eyes willing me to drop something edible.

"Slow down, you're going to chew off one of your fingers, if you're not careful." my mother insisted.

I just smiled at her, unable to reply because of the mass of food in my mouth, I waggled my butter smeared digits at her ... and all ten were all still there.

**** .

The sun was casting two short shadows as we walked up Brendon Avenue, me with Edward slung loosely over my shoulder like a 'swag' bag, Stew was directly in front of me, but walking backwards as he spoke.

"Aww, go on, it'll be brilliant." he begged.

"No chance, you are not using Edward in a knife throwing act!" I said firmly.

"But why not? He's not real, I can sorta understand you not letting me use Trumper, but Edward, he's just a wooden doll!" he flung his arms wide as he spoke.

"He isn't 'just' a wooden doll ... he's like a friend." I tried to explain how close me and my wooden pal were.

"I thought I was your best friend." he said this as the bag he carried jangled with two of his mother's carving knives and a dagger so large, Paul Hogan would borrow it years later for a scene in Crocodile Dundee. I shivered at the thought of him flinging them through the air at my dummy.

We turned onto McConnell Road, we were just minutes from the venue, that's when I felt the nerves really kick in, my mouth became a little dryer, and my stomach tightened a touch.

"Do you remember all the questions?" I asked.

"Course I do." confidence was escaping my body from every pore with each step closer we got to the theatre. I pondered why my pal feared so few things, I decided he had probably been dropped on his head at a very young age, a type of non-invasive frontal lobotomy ... that would actually explain an awful lot of Stewart's peculiar traits.

There, on the other side of Kenyon Lane stood the theatre, a single storey building, built in a dark brown brick. Over the double front doors was a large wooden sign advertising the talent contest about to take place, and on the steps and all around the front was an informal queue. Once we identified ourselves as competitors we were fast tracked passed the crowd and gained access into the building.

We went and had a look at the list of acts and the times they would be performing, there was a juggler, a couple of singers. One of them was Jan van Klomp, a South African boy who had only joined Stewarts class at Lily Lane last term, there was also a girls dance troupe from the Julia Octavio School of Dance, 'The Eight Little Darlings'. Looking around I could spot all the darlings, eight young girls with giant blonde, Dolly Parton wigs stuck on their tiny heads, sequined mini dresses that exposed the biggest, frilliest knickers I had ever seen and white tap socks and tap shoes on their tiny feet.

There were seven acts altogether, I was second last after Holly Hopday, a pretty blonde girl that had took my eye at school, she was going to sing and if I didn't win, I wanted her to. The merest hint of testosterone had filtered into my bloodstream over the last few months and she was my first real crush.

"Anybody who is performing, can they make their way to the front." a large man, in a red checked shirt, called above the hubbub.

Me and Stew, wandered forward, Stew's knives were rattling noisily as we walked. I was carrying Edward on my left forearm, my right hand was jammed up his backside, his wooden eyes were exceedingly wide, it was as if he was startled by the intrusion.

"Flipping 'eck, I'm getting nervous." I whispered.

"What about?"

"What do you mean, what about? About flaming sitting up there in front of everybody!" I said louder.

"Piece of cake, it'll be funny."

"You've only got to remember some questions … I've got to remember the answers and not move my lips, and have everybody looking at me."

"Just imagine they are all naked then!" he casually suggested.

"What!" I twisted my head and stared at him.

"Just think of them naked, you won't be scared then."

"How does that work? Sitting up in front of 100 or so naked Mostonians, how is that supposed to be a calming experience?"

"Don't know … but I do it all the time. You've got no clothes on right now!" he said with a smile.

"What? Stoppit … you really are weird, do you know that? Proper potty!" I pulled Edward across the front of my trousers.

"That's not fair … I'm not potty, just a little eccentric."

"Not potty!!!? Three 'maffis' knives in a plastic bag … annnnnd you regularly imagine people naked when you talk to them … I think I'm being more than fair calling you potty!" I shook my head dismissively as I turned back to listen to the man with the clipboard.

"One of my teachers said I was an extraordinary boy!" he whispered into my ear.

"What does that even mean?" I asked without turning.

"Errm...well...there's ordinary...like what you are," he gestured my way, "...and then there's extra...ordinary, that's normal … with a bit more...ouch!" he had tried to fold his arms but had succeeded in stabbing himself as the bag swung and hit his leg.

"A bit more what? A bit more mad, a bit more danger, a bit more..." I struggled for another word to describe his mindset.

"...imagination!" he claimed.

"Well I can't argue with that, you do have the weirdest ideas." In the end I had to accept he really was extra...ordinary.

"Boys, boys, come on. Now, who are you, what are you doing." the chubby guy asked, the queue had dissipated and we were now at the front.

"Brian Hamblett and Edward Woodhead, the Miraculous Memory Man. I stated proudly.

"Are you Brian?"

"Yes."

"You must be Edward then!" he looked at Stewart.

"No."

"Well, who are you?" he flipped at his paperwork furiously.

"Stewart."

"Stewart...?" he looked again at the clipboard in his hand. "I don't have a Stewart ... you're not on here." panic caused his larynx to tighten and his voice rose girlishly.

"No, I'm just helping, carrying some stuff for him." he lifted the bag of knives.

"Oh. Thank God for that, I thought I'd missed you off the list." his voice had fallen back to a more masculine tone. "Right, go through there, boys changing rooms to the right." he pulled the curtain directly behind him to the side, revealing a door. We squeezed past him and opened the door, the first thing that hit you was the noise, the sound of songs being test run, the squealing of excited little girls, and the rhythmic clatter of tap shoes on wood.

44

In the drab dressing room, two boys were there, Jan, pronounced Yan, was sat on a bench, his jacket on a hook above him. In the middle of the room was a ginger lad who was doing a run through of a Ceili, a traditional Irish dance. We stopped and stared at him, his body was as rigid as a tree trunk with his arms stuck to his side, but his legs flew out and up, across and round, all at the speed of light! And he was wearing clogs while he did it! It was as if his top half of his body had gone into rigor mortis but his legs were having an epileptic fit.

"What's the flaming hell is he doing?" I asked quietly.

"I'll be buggered if I know." Stew replied with the small rattle of his knives as he shrugged his shoulders.

"Well, you can't win a talent contest by doing something that isn't a talent ... just flinging your legs around ... he just looks completely bonkers." I stated. "Here hold Edward, I'm just going to the lav." I passed my wooden friend over to my 'extraordinary' friend and headed for the door in the corner of the room with a stick man painted on it.

I opened the toilet door and flicked the light switch, nothing happened, I looked up at the unlit bulb, I tried the switch twice more with exactly the same result. I tutted and used the light flooding in from behind me to gain an idea of the positioning of the toilet bowl. I reluctantly closed and locked the door then undid my trousers, they fell and I sat down in the gloom, the seat was both cold and damp, making me shiver.

When all my ablutions were well and truly done, I grasped in the dark for where I suspected the toilet paper would be to my right … nothing, just wall. I ran my hand up and down in desperation, still no luck. I leaned to my left and tried again, upwards, sidewards then downwards … again nothing. I started to grow desperate, I rummaged on the floor, in a semicircular motion from one side of the toilet bowl to the other, and found a couple of loose pieces of paper. Relief flooded my body, slowly I tore the A4 sheets in half and although it was a little firm to the touch, I was able to do what was required.

I pulled up my trousers, fastened buttons and belt then turned and flushed, eventually I unlocked the door, the light that hit me when I exited made me half close my eyes.

"Hey man, can you pass me my sheets out of there, pliz." a South African voice requested,

"Pardon?" I asked, panic setting in.

"My song sheets, man, I left them in there, bring them out with you." no please from him now.

I looked at the boy, I say boy but he was twice as large as me, and just a year older. He had the beginning of facial hair on his chin and top lip, at 11!!

"I'm sorry, I don't see any sheets in there…" I turned and opened the toilet door, bent inwards and desperately hoped his song sheets were on the floor. Something caught my eye in the toilet bowl, there floating and stained by the use it had been put to, was a song sheet. I froze for a second, then quickly lent further in and pulled the chain again, praying for it to disappear round the U bend. Once the water settled, so did the torn piece of a song sheet, crumpled and discoloured.

"What you doin, man?" the man-boy asked.

"I've got a floater, just trying to sink it, this is very embarrassing." I stammered.

"My sheets, man, they are definitely in there, for sure."

"No. Nothing here, matey," I said as I lifted a toilet brush, and plunged it towards the floating paper … trying desperately to push the evidence down, jamming it towards the bend. "Nope, are you sure it's not out there with you?" I said over my shoulder.

"Hey, I told you, it's in there." his voice was getting closer and louder. I reached up and pulled on the chain again and at the same time repeated a fast plunging action with my other hand, water splashing up onto my hand.

I was yanked backwards and gave a yelp, the big South African took my place in the doorway. He pushed the door fully open and stared intently, his head moving slowly like oil tanker turning mid ocean.

"Where the…" he said in his throaty Boer accent.

"I know … it's not there, and I looked everywhere, it's just a mystery Jan, you probably know the words to the song anyway, so not really a problem, hey?

"I need them, what have you done with them?" his accusing eyes staring into my very soul.

"Me....? What could I have done with them? Search me!" I opened my arms wide to show I wasn't hiding them.

He faced me full on now, and his face was full of hate. I felt a shiver run from the nape of my neck the full length of my spine.

"If I find you have hidden them, I will pull your leg off and eat it!" he said this slowly so as to get the full implications of there being any shenanigans on my part.

"Eat my leg?!!!" I asked. "You want to eat my leg?" had I misunderstood his broad accent?

"I will take your little girl doll there," he pointed at Edward, "set it on fire and cook your leg over it!" nope, nothing had been lost in translation...

"Jan, why would I want to do anything to your lovely music?" my arms were still spread, my head was leaning slightly to one side, trying to be as disarming as possible, Christ-like even.

He walked towards me, lifted an arm, I crumpled, ready for the killer blow. He just pushed me to the floor and stormed out, muttering in what I now suspect was, Afrikaans.

I lifted my head and breathed deeply, glad to be alive. I slowly looked around the dressing room, the ginger lad was smiling broadly at me, looking slightly mad. I nodded in his direction.

There was sign of Stewart, but there was Edward, sat on a blue, plastic chair in the opposite corner. I got to my feet and walked over to him ... I stopped short, there was something sticking out of Edwards forehead. It was a large carving knife!

"What the…." I raced over and grabbed the knife, it was almost all the way through his head. I pulled the knife, but only succeeded in yanking Edwards head upwards, revealing the pole and the wire I used to manipulate his jaw with. It was stuck solid, there was no removing the knife no matter how I hard I tugged.

"Martin? Martin Feeney…" the tubby man was staring down at his clipboard again, "You're up in 10 minutes. Julie, the juggling gymnast is just about to start, then it's … erm … Jan … Yan? Then you" he explained, while pouring over his paperwork.

"Excuse me, mister, have you seen my friend, Stewart?" I asked before he left.

"Is that the dark haired boy, with the skinny legs, and abnormally large knees?" he questioned.

"That's him, where is he?"

"I asked him to fill some balloons with helium, he shouldn't be long." he was walking through the door before he finished the sentence, much too busy to chat with a scruffy little kid like me.

I sat on the chair, Edward was sat on my knee, lifeless, legs swinging ever so slowly, arms dangling at his side and a large carving knife jammed four inches into his skull through his forehead. All that was missing was several pints of blood and blue flashing lights of a Black Maria. I knew the victim and I was pretty sure who the assassin was.

49

"Your mate…" I had heard the ginger boy clip clopping across the room on his way to the stage, I looked up as he spoke.

"Pardon."

"It was your mate, he was throwing knives at you doll, I think it was an accident though, he squealed like a girl when he hit your dolls head" he smiled that empty smile again, then left the room, clip clopping like a giant Pinocchio.

"Stew! I knew it!" I fumed, "Knife flipping throwing, I'll flaming give him knife throwing!"

I got myself together, straightened Edward as best I could, and checked his mouth mechanism still worked. My finger pulled at the wooden switch attached to the pole, the head sat on the pole and fed through the neck into his guts. I had to insert my hand in through a gap in his jacket to reach the pole. Another switch allowed me to make him blink. Both switches were working fine, he just looked like a murder victim.

From outside, I could hear the most beautiful voice, angelic almost. It was 'Something', the song made famous by the Beatles. There were no bum notes and there was even a hint of McCartney about the performance, when the song finished a few seconds later the audience erupted, you could hear the squeal of chairs being pushed back as they rose to proclaim his efforts.

The curtains suddenly pulled sideways and the giant Boer shoved his way through, my jaw dropped. Surely that singing could not have come from that face!

He walked towards me in a heavy legged stomp, he caught my eye and with that glance I knew I was to move out of the doorway, to let him through to his seat in the changing room. I stepped sideways and smiled.

"See, you didn't need your song sheet, you were brilliant." I said with a slight quiver to my voice.

"I don't trust you, boy, so stay out of my way ... forever!" the angelic tone of his singing had certainly been left on stage, and the gruff, throaty accent was back. I felt like Jack after climbing the Beanstalk ... and there a South African giant could smell the blood of an Englishman...erm...boy.

He disappeared into the room to my relief, I certainly wasn't going back in there on my own with him, so I crept quietly to the curtains edge and peeped round. On stage was the ginger boy with the clogs on, and next to him was the compere, he was asking him questions about his dancing style. Apparently this was a traditional Irish dance and he had previously won prizes in lots of dancing competitions. Before I could hear any more I felt a tap on my shoulder. I turned to see the biggest, bluest eyes looking up at me.

"Hello Brian, what's your friend called?" it was Holly Hobday, blonde, blue eyed and seriously pretty.

"He's called Stew, you know him, I think!" I stuttered slightly.

"Not that friend, this one." she put her porcelain finger on Edwards nose.

"Oh, oh...er...this is...I...erm." I just stood looking at Edward and was unable to recall his name, this

51

was the start of what I like to call girl amnesia, something I would suffer with for the next ten years or so.

"He he. You've forgot your dummy's name! Are you nervous?" she asked in that sing song voice of hers.

"I am … I'm flaming terrified." The stage fright was as much just talking to her, as it was going on stage.

"You'll be fine, you're funny and they'll love you." she smiled.

In my head I was screaming...'can you love me too, please?' My cheeks took on the colour of two illuminated brake lights. What the flipping heck was going on with me? I didn't even like girls, they're soppy and play with dolls. Saying that, I think Jan van Klomp had said the same about me, to be honest.

"Are, are you on next, Hobby … erm, bugger … I mean Hoddy … Holly … yes, Holly?" my stuttering was getting worse.

"You are funny, calm down and take a deep breath." she said.

I decided just to smile, the conversation thing was going to end up with me just looking completely mad.

"Should we just watch the dancer?" she whispered and pulled the curtain back so we could see along the stage.

The music started and it was an Irish pipe and whistle 'de diddly diddly' sort of tune. Martin was stood rigid again from the waist up and his legs were going ten to the dozen, they had taken on their own life...forwards and up, backwards and down, his feet together on the stage knitting in and out with tripping himself up, then he flung the right foot up towards the left hand stuck to his side. The heel of the foot made contact with his hand and a loud scream erupted from his mouth, his legs suddenly stopped and Martin bent in two, he gripped his left hand. Blood began oozing through the fingers, and the low moan started emanating from deep inside him.

A woman at the front, I suspect it was his mother, called out his name as she clambered onto the stage in an undignified manner, she had hitched her long skirt up to her lower buttocks, exposing the tops of her tights and thighs, but this mattered little ... her boy was in distress and crying.

"Oh dear." Holly gasped, "I hope he's alright, there's an awful lot of blood."

"Seems daft dancing in clogs, if you don't hurt yourself, you're just gonna hurt someone else." I suggested.

"It's Ceili dancing, they all dance in clogs!"

"Bet there's quite a bloodbath when they're all dancing together, be like United and City fans fighting at a football match." my mind drifted to a possible scenario on the Stretford End, an enormous dance off between two set of fans in clogs, each taking it in turns to sing a song and clog dance while thousands of the opposing fans stood, hands on hips waiting their turn to clip clop a tune right back, be much better than fighting ... and probably the football too!

"Oh here's your friend." she looked to my right as she said this. I turned to see Stew, sprinting with a gas canister the size of a small fire extinguisher in his hand, he had a look of terror on his face.

"Oh hello … would you like to explain this…?" I pointed at Edwards forehead, knife embedded to the hilt.

"Hide me..." it was Stews mouth, but he was using the voice of Mickey Mouse.

"What the…" I stared at his lips. Holly burst out laughing, lifting her hand to cover her mouth.

"That dance teacher, she's gonna kill me." he said, again in Mickey's voice.

"What've you done? To the teacher … and your flipping voice?" I demanded.

"It wasn't me," his voice was beginning to return to a more human timbre, "the dance girls asked to have a go, I never made 'em" he blurted out, while trying to get his breath.

"Oh no, what have you done to them?" I wailed.

"I just let 'em have a drag on the helium ... and if they kept asking, well that's not my fault, is it?

"Did their voices gone funny?"

"It did, but two of 'em were sick and asked to go home. That dance teacher's screaming blue murder, saying she's gonna strangle me."

The tubby compere-organiser appeared through the centre of the main stage curtains backstage. The gap had been found in the style of Eric Morecambe, a desperate bashing of the drapes until a hand found the separation and pulled apart to allow a weeping boy dancer and a mother bent down trying to give consolation. His wounded hand was visible and the

54

thumb was sticking out at an irregular angle suggesting a dislocation.

"You're up next…" he looked at the clipboard, "Holly." he guided the two Feeney's towards the dressing room where Martins civilian clothes were.

"Oooh, it's me Brian, you going to wish me luck?" she asked.

"Erm, yes, of course, good luck…" I stuck out a hand.

"What a numpty!" Stew said in exasperation.

"Shut it you! We have a head … and a knife to talk about!" I barked in his face.

"Calm down, Hammy, you know it was an accident. I just had a quick go at knife throwing and it went straight through his head, it could've happened to anyone!" he protested.

"And you wanted to use Trumper! How was that going to end up? Me with a dead dog? You with a prison sentence?"

"I'm too young to go to jail. They've said they'll have to wait a few years until they can actually lock me up."

Clipboard guy came back and guided Holly to the centre of the stage, behind the main curtain, they stepped over a mop and bucket, he grabbed the microphone from the stand, took a breath then pushed into the drapes.

"And we're are back ladies and gentlemen." there was a ripple of applause and he continued to question Holly on her hopes and desires.

"Right, we will sort this out later, we need to get ready for our performance." I said more calmly.

"I was thinking, what if we changed it? Slightly." Stew suggested.

"Whatttt? Now? Three minutes before I go on? You really are a nutcase."

"I've found a torch … and with this helium it'll be really funny." he explained.

"No..no...no...I'm going to have a heart attack! Stop it now. Just go out, ask Edward the questions and I'll give the answers, we will bow...the crowd will…"

"....be asleep!" Stew interrupted.

"How can we change it now?" in the background Holly began singing Good Ship Lollypop.

"You, you boy." Stewart's ear was grabbed by a furious looking dance teacher.

"Argggghhhh! Let go." Stew squealed. The tubby guy, accidently kicked the bucket as he returned.

"What's up now?" he asked, perplexed.

"This feral youth has poisoned two of my girls, I want him removed from the premises immediately." she said in a posh accent.

"Poisoned, oh no, are they dead?" he nearly dropped his paperwork in shock...

"No, of course not, silly man, they have been vomiting and are just about to leave for home. This idiot boy made them inhale helium, so stupid, I am two girls short now, and we won't be able to perform now."

"Don't chuck him out, he's part of my act … I can't go on without him, and I haven't done anything wrong." I begged.

"That is not my problem little boy, you can thank your friend here, he's spoilt our show too, so you can blame him." she crossed her arms belligerently.

"What if me and Bri take the girls places?" Stew asked.

"You whatttt?!!!" I blurted out.

"We can go on and copy the girls. The show must go on, hey?" he shrugged his shoulders.

"I can't dance, you certainly can't dance, and we will just look silly, two boys with all them girls." Miss Julia, rubbed her chin and looked thoughtful for a second.

"I could supply two dresses, and you could each go on the very end of the line, if you," she turned to clipboard man, "could close the main curtains slightly, they could be slightly hidden, and I have eight girls again." she pondered.

"Dresses? Dresses? I not wearing no dress, take him to jail...I give in, take me to jail too...dancing in a dress...in front of people...people I may actually know...no flipping way!!!" I stuttered, stammered and looked from Stew to Julia the dance teacher.

"Oh stop over reacting you drama queen, you'll be wearing a wig and make up, no one will recognise you, for goodness sake." she said dismissively.

"Oh, make up and a wig, well that's okay then! No problem." I said sarcastically.

"It'll be fun, Hammy, bit of a laugh." Stew tried to talk me round.

"It will not be a bit of fun, little boy, you will take it serious, you have had enough fun at my expense, you thug." clipboard guy's head was going to and fro trying to work out what was happening, meanwhile, Holly was coming to the end of her song.

"Right, are you going on then, or not?" he asked me.

"NO...erm. Yes...but...a dress...a dress!!"

He walked to the middle of the main stage curtain, and picked the mic of the stand, and waited for the song to finish, preparing to push through.

"I'll go and get your dresses ready..." Miss Julia muttered as she walked away.

"You are ruining my life!!" I half shouted at Stew, he just smiled.

"Like she said, stop over reacting, in 15 minutes, it'll all be over."

"My life will be over! You just go and get ready for our act, get out there." I pointed towards the audience sat behind the curtain out of view.

"I'll go out when he announces you."

"Go now."

"I need a wee!"

"Oh, for God's sake." I was on the verge of collapse.

"Calm down, it's just a wee, not a poo!" Stew said trying to calm me.

"Oh yippedy do dah ... it's just a wee." I threw my free arm in the air.

"I'll do it in that bucket when you go on."

"In the mop bucket, why not go to the loo now?"

"I don't want to! The bucket'll be fine, and I'll get out straight after."

"Pointless arguing with you, isn't it?"

"Yep!!" he smiled his lipless smile.

There was a swishing and flailing of curtains then Holly appeared. She had a big smile on her face, obviously pleased with her performance.

"Did you see me?"

"Yes, you were brilliant." I lied.

"You didn't see her!" Stew said, looking bemused.

"I didn't...erm...see you, but I listened, I didn't want to put you off by popping my head round the curtain." I tried to explain, I sent my best laser stare at Stewart.

"Did you? I thought you were moaning about having to wear a dress." he said this while he backed away.

"Stewart ... will you just shut up, please? I did listen Holly, and you have a lovely voice."

"Brian and Edward ... come on, you're going on." he gestured us towards him.

I followed him, stepping over Stew's soon to be potty, and nervously walked through on to the stage. There was a chair now placed centrally for me to sit on, and a microphone to be positioned once I sat down.

"Ladies and gentlemen, this is Brian from...?" he shoved the mike under my nose.

"Lakin Street."

"Oh, yes just off Lightbowne Road?"

"Errr yeah."

"What school do you go to, Brian?"

"Lily Lane Junior School."

"Ha-ha, just across the road there." he pointed in the general direction to where my school lay over the road from this theatre...

"Okay, Brian, what are you going to do for us today?"

"Right, erm, me and my friend...erm...Edward," I lifted my dummy up with my right hand and sat him on my left arm.

"What's the knife in his head for?" a shout from the crowd.

"Gentlemen, calm down, I'm sure it's all part of the act, hey Brian?"

"Nope, me mate threw a knife at him ... and I can't get it out!"

There was a massive laugh from the crowd.

"Are you sure it's not an attempted suicide?" same voice from out front.

"Please guys, give him a chance. Should we carry on? This is Brian and his friend Edward, the amazing Memory Man." he promptly turned and abandoned me. I sat down, moved the microphone to my mouth, and coughed.

"Hello ladies and gentlemen, my name is Brian and this is Edward..." suddenly over the sound system came the sound of someone urinating into a tin vessel. This was loud and backed by someone young obviously relieved to be emptying their bladder. I had stopped talking and was gazing upwards, the sound of giggling from the audience was building.

The urinating went on...and on and on. It suddenly stopped, there was a large, 'ahhhhhhhhhh,' followed almost instantly by an 'oooh' and it began again. I looked over my shoulder at the curtain and Edward looked back with me.

The crowd were laughing very loudly now, Edwards mouth was just opening and shutting silently. Then the urinating suddenly stopped.

"Don't forget to flush!" someone shouted creating another uproar. "...and wash your hands, you dirty devil!"

"I...er...okay...back to me, I think...this is Edward. And what do you do, Edward?" I looked at my wooden doll with a knife in his head.

"I an a memory man." he replied with a chomping jaw, whilst my teeth were clamped together. Most of Edwards's words were mispronounced.

"Oh, ladies and gentlemen, he's a memory man. So do you know everything?" I quizzed.

"I goo! Gwel, almost hevryfink!" pronunciation was getting worse and my lips were not at all static. Then the lights in the hall went out, and a torch light flashed on through the curtains to my rear, the beam landed on people in the crowd, then moved slowly across them.

"This is the voice of the Mysterons ... we know you can hear us Earthmen..." it was Stew, a deeper version of his voice, but it was definitely him. The laughing was getting louder. "...we have not forgotten what you did and so we intend to destroy Moston!"

"Start with the Ben Brierley Pub! I might get my husband home for his tea once in a while, ha ha..." a woman had piped up from the back, through the gloom.

"This has nothing to do with me" I had leaned forward and whispered into the microphone.

"Edward, this is the voice of the Mysterons and we will ask you five questions. And only if you get them all correct will you save Moston! Get them wrong and we will destroy it ... little by little!" the torch was still wandering around the audience.

I looked round at the curtain and could see Stew's hand holding the torch through the gap. I was tempted to jump up and pull him through, but fear kept my backside rooted to the chair.

"Question one, Edward, which book begins with the words ... Call me Ishmael?"

This was the first of the questions we had agreed on, so I began manipulating Edwards's mechanism, his jaw began its up and down motion.

"Jer ansher ish Moby Jick!" the ventriloquist doll answered with his unique speech impediment.

"Lucky answer Earthling with wooden head." a cheer went up.

"Question two, what year was the Magna Carta signed?

"Jer ansher to that queshtion ish...erm...shwelve hifteen." I was in the groove now. These were the questions we had practiced so best just go with the flow.

"Arghhh...you are a clever doll, Edward, you are right again, but I do not think you will get this one as easy." the deep voice uttered from the ether. The crowd was now in hysterics, cheering when the confirmation of another correct answer and asking each other what the dummy was actually saying.

"Well done, Edward, I never realised that you were so clever!" I said to my doll in a staccato, bad actor tone.

"I'm not azz fick azz you look." he replied to me, mouth opening and shutting willy nilly, eyes blinking at ten to the dozen. I tried to look shocked at his cheek.

"Question three Earthman. How many pints are there in a firkin?" the Mysteron asked.

"Jer are sheventy chew pints in a furkkin, ju alien menace!" I was beginning to enjoy this.

"Oooooo, three firkins and a packet of cheese and onion down here, please ... ha ha." a large man three rows back shouted, they were loving it now and they were getting quite raucous.

"Quiet, scumbags, or I will marmalize you all!" Stew threatened from behind the curtain. Pointing the torch at the latest heavyweight offender.

"Fourth question ... you cannot win, Memory man, Moston will be mine!"

"Jats not a queshtion, is it?" Edward asked the alien.

"No, course it's not, idiot." Stew said in his real voice. "Errr. Question four, who created the Great Western Railway?" reverting back to the deep, menacing tones of the Mysterons.

"Jat would ge … Ishhemgard Kingjom Grunel." a garbled but confident answer came from my timber friend.

"Drat you, you wooden genius, you are right again." he said dramatically.

The cheers were getting really loud now, chants of 'Moston' and 'we hate the Mysterons' were popping up between each question.

"Well done again, Edward, one more question right and you've saved the Earth." I said happily to my dummy.

"It's not the whole Earth, Hammy. I'm only gonna blow up flippin' Moston." Stew said over the sound system, in his own childlike, high pitched voice.

"Jesh, I'm just gonna shave Goston." Edward agreed.

"Last question, get this right and your town is safe, get it wrong and you will all be smashed to smithereens." he said menacingly. "So … to not die an 'orrible death … who was Walt Disney's first cartoon character?" I looked bemused, where was the Everest question? The one we had agreed on, why had he suddenly changed it?

"Come on, Edward, save us … save us all from a marmalization." a cry went up.

My mind was blank, then I heard the hiss of gas just behind the curtain. What was he doing now? Then I realised, it was Disney's favourite character.

"Jer ansher, and joo shave jer World ish … Mickey Mouse!" the mass of people in front of me erupted. Over the tannoy came the reaction from our evil inquisitor. But this time he was talking in that high pitched, helium induced voice. And if you closed your eyes it was actually Mickey himself.

"That's all folks ... he he he" not a Disney tag line, but it seemed to work fine.

Clipboard guy pushed through onto the stage, then popped his head back to ask to have the lights turned back on.

"There you go ladies and gentlemen, Brian and Edward, he paused for applause. People pushed their chairs back and stood. I stood myself, bowed and then made Edward bow. The biggest roar was when Stew stuck his head through and said 'hiya folks' into his microphone in the helium enhanced voice.

We were guided off stage while he explained there would be a little delay while the next act got ready, making me realise I had to flipping dance.

"Hey, we might win." Stew said in Mickey's voice, I couldn't concentrate on what he was saying, just how he was saying it.

"What were you thinking, just changing it at the last minute."

"I was thinking we might win if I did!" he grinned

"Boys here, put these on. There's a dress, socks and a wig ... and these large frilly knickers." Miss Julia had been waiting for us.

"Oh no, I'm not wearing frilly knickers." I insisted.

"You'll have to, you have to bend over at the end of the song and show your backside."

"This is mental, what are girls showing there bums for anyway, isn't it a bit rude?

"Don't be pathetic boy, it's a little bit of fun, that's all." she said dismissively, they are little girls, not can can dancers. Now move it, chop chop."

"I do not believe this, why is it always me?" I said as we walked away.

"I bet I make a prettier girl than you!" Stew said to me.

"I hope you blinking do."

"You're too heavy, you've got fat legs." he explained.

"Shut up. You want taking away in a white van."

We walked in the changing room, sat opposite us was Jan van Klomp, he was staring at us.

"I'm not getting changed in front of that gorilla!" I whispered to Stew.

"Why not?"

"Oh, I don't know, maybe because I will look like a freak."

"You worry too much."

"I worry about you, and almost certainly not enough. I'm getting changed outside." I did an about turn and looked for a bit of privacy.

I found a chair with a towel on it near to the back wall, I looked around and it looked deserted. Quickly I took off my blue tee shirt and hung it over the back of the chair, I wrapped the towel round my waist, kicked off my shoes and undid my shorts. I struggled one hand holding the towel, the other pulling my shorts down, constantly shaking my head and saying 'I don't believe this.'

Eventually I stepped out of them and held up the white dress that sparkled and shimmered with sequins, I shook my head. I put both legs inside and pulled it up, the towel fell downwards to the floor, I put the dress on my shoulders and realised I would need help zipping it up so I put the large white wig on my head and pulled it down to my ears, twisting and turning it until it felt like it wasn't going to fall off.

"Hey, Hammy … look at me." it was Stew, he looked way too feminine for his own good.

"Good God, why are you enjoying this?" I asked.

"It's all good fun, here I'll zip you up." he walked over and lifted his arms in readiness.

"Don't catch me skin, be careful."

"You should go on a diet." he pulled slowly on the zip, it pulled my flab in as it got higher.

"Do you want me to do yours?" I offered.

"Already done, I got Jan to help."

"Didn't he say anything?"

"He did, but I'll be buggered if I could understand a word he said."

"Boys here, I will just run you through what I want you to do, it's simple, the girls will be tapping, you move your legs in time with theirs." she explained the routine as best she could. I was completely lost, why anybody thought this was a good idea was completely beyond me. Stew just smiled inanely, like a fairy had granted him his greatest wish.

When the other girls joined us there was an awful lot of giggling, they pointed at my puppy fat, my hairy legs and Stews hint of a pubescent moustache. We were objects of mockery, my life would never be the same, I could feel the scars on my self-esteem, they were there for life...they would never heal.

The next five minutes were a blur, I had complained about the bloomers cutting off the blood to my legs and stomach, a set of little scissors nicked the elastic, loosening them ever so slightly.

We stood in a line behind the curtain, six young girls all about the same height, at one end of the line standing a good foot taller was me, weighing the same as three of the dancers, Stew was at the other end, slightly taller but blending in so much better than me and grinning like the Cheshire Cat.

"Right guy's, I'll go through and announce you to the audience, the curtains will draw back and the music will start, you all okay with that?" asked the chubby compere.

All the girls including Stew nodded with excitement, I let my head drop, no eye contact with anyone, I just wanted this over, and hopefully I wouldn't be recognised.

The compere introduced us, the music started, Puppet on a String by Sandie Shaw then the curtains pulled back revealing the six girls and two young transvestites, one deliriously happy and then there was me, totally suicidal. Within four seconds the cry went up 'It's that Brian … look, on the end. What's he doing dancing with the girls?' I moved more to my right, trying to hide, there was loud laughter and lots of fingers pointing at me.

The girls started tap dancing in rhythm, moving like clockwork, arms swinging in tandem, large grins spread across their faces. I tried my best, I really did, but if you think of the hippo ballet dancer in Fantasia, then take any of that cartoon characters dance talent away, then you basically have me. I stared to my left constantly, trying to keep my legs in time with theirs, with little or no success…meanwhile Stewart, much to the amusement of the crowd, did his own dance, a version of the Can Can, bringing the Moulin Rouge to Moston. Half way through an arm reached from behind the curtain slowly, then and pulled him off stage, this starting some booing.

I wandered as much out of view as possible, but there was no exit on my side of the stage, and even worse the knicker elastic had broken completely and I was having to hold them up with one hand while I bounced around. That was it … enough was enough … so I started dancing behind the girls, moving left, towards an angry looking Miss Julia, slowly but surely I got closer to an exit, I pulled the curtain apart and disappeared.

Once I was behind the curtain, Julia chastised me in sign language, finger wagging, then hands on hips. I just bent down and removed my frilly knickers, I straightened up and handed them back to her. Then, summoning up what little dignity was left in my self-respect bank, I walked off, looking for my boys clothes.

69

We all congregated back on stage ten minutes later to hear the results, Stew stood in the wings, worryingly still in the sparkly dance dress! When I caught his eye, he gave me double thumbs up, I gave him a small shake off my head...and mouthed the words 'no chance.'

The compere told us he had collected the voting slips from the judges at the rear, whom he introduced individually so they could each receive a small ripple of applause. Six of the seven acts were lined up taking up most of the stage, Martin had gone to Crumpsall Hospital to have his thumb relocated. Each act was reintroduced before the results were announced, we stood forward to take our applause as we were called. The man thanked us for our efforts and entertainment, which again gave reason for the crowd to applaud.

Finally he took a deep breath…

"So ladies and gentlemen, I now come to the results, and in third place Holly Hobday…" Holly did a little jig of joy, her golden locks bouncing, this all happened in slow motion in my eyes. She walked up to receive her prize, a small silver cup the size of an egg cup and a certificate of some sort. The audience kept clapping while this went on.

"In second place and this was close, ladies and gentlemen, was our first act of the evening, the juggling gymnast … Julie Pole, well done Julie." again the handshake, the silver cup, a little larger this time, and the certificate. She looked a little disappointed but managed to force a smile.

"Well, it's time to announce our winner now, but before I announce them don't forget the new Musical that starts here next week ... Five Brides for Five Brothers, erm, this a scaled down version of the Film and West End show apparently, I would assume not enough actors available." apparently unsure to the loss of two brothers and their potential spouses. He lifted the clipboard and looked down, smiled and nodded his head, obviously agreeing with the judge's choice. "The winner this year is....." I looked side stage at Stew, who had lifted his white wig slightly to allow room to stick fingers in his ears, his eyes were tight shut, like he was expecting one of his occasional firework experiments to bring down the building.

"...Jan ... van ... Klomp!" he said loudly, four sad balloons fell from above, Stew collapsed to his bulbous knees, shaking his head so hard his wig fell off, he was obviously distraught. Jan walked forward to grab the prize givers hand, who seemed to wince at the powerful young boys grip.

"Think you, think you everybody." he had grabbed the microphone and was shouting into it, making clipboard guy lose his congratulatory smile. The crowd were clapping and undoubtedly in agreement with the result.

I turned and headed stage left, where I passed a Stew in the foetal position on the floor.

"Come on, it's time to go home matey."

"We was robbed! No, I was robbed!" he garbled.

"We were hoomiliated ... shown up ... we were rubbish and it's all your fault."

"Meeeee!!" he was looking up now from his prostrate position.

"Oh, yes, you!! You are the worst best mate possible, I had to wear a dress! What if someone's taken a photo? What if any one our friends saw us?

But ... what if we'd actually won?" Stew interceded.

"But...we...didn't. We lost." I said this slowly hoping he would finally understand.

"Only just!"

"We weren't even in the top three of seven! Where ... one act broke his thumb after twenty seconds and walked off crying ... annnnnd not only that, there was an eight girl tap dancing act that only had six girls! They had two boys in dresses with them, one who did a completely different dance to everyone else!" I shook my head at the memory. "And then there was me! The dancer who looked like she had suddenly turned into the Incredible Hulk ... or Dr. Jekyll!" I raged.

"Mr. Hyde..."

"What?"

"Doctor Jekyll was normal ... Mr. Hyde was the monster. Everyone makes that mistake.

"Does it matter? I looked completely stupid, my knickers were falling down ... I actually danced off the stage trying to hold up my frilly, flipping, knickers."

"I know, but...."

72

"But nothing! We were rubbish ... let's go home." I turned and walked away. "And don't think I'm walking back with you in that blinking dress!" I barked.

"I'm not stupid!" he said, obviously walking home in a dress was too much even for Stewart Neale.

I turned back to him and just stared. We were going to be the laughing stock of Moston, thank God my mother had to work today and my dad was in Leicester with his lorry.

I looked for a door we could leave from in anonymity at the rear of the building while he changed, under no circumstances did I want to be recognised by the throng out front. Stew appeared with his bag of knives and dressed like a street urchin again ... back to normality.

"Here, we can escape through this fire door, climb over the wall onto Bluestone Road, then get onto Edale and hope no one will see us."

"Okay, good idea." he agreed.

I pushed open the door, then slowly peeked out. It was devoid of people, so we made our getaway, me carrying Edward, still with a knife in his head, Stew close behind with his jangling bag. We clambered over the wall and started away from the theatre, walking quickly, me in front.

"You're still me mate, aren't you?" Stew asked perkily, almost a laugh in his voice.

"I don't know, you've made me look an utter baboon!" I shouted, walking faster than him.

"What? A baboon? I've made you look like a monkey with a red arse?" he called after me.

"It's what my Dad says. It means idiot too." I tried to explain.

"I think you mean buffoon?" he started to catch me up.

"Errr, that's it ... baboon ... buffoon … does it matter? A red face or a red bum either way I lose." I said without looking back.

"Please be my mate!" this time it was Mickey Mouse asking, I turned to see Stew with the small bottle of helium, grinning wide.

I couldn't suppress my laughter, my anger would have to be put on the shelf for now, along with the multitude of other annoyances that had yet to be dealt with.

"You've nicked the helium? You can't keep nicking stuff, Stew."

"I've just 'lent' it." he squeaked. "Do you want a go?" he proffered the canister towards me. I stopped and looked at it, my brain saying no, but my hand deciding yes.

"What do I do?"

"Put this in your mouth Pluto … and I'll turn the tap" it arrived at my lips, there was a hiss and cold gas arrived in my mouth.

"Now swallow!"

I did as I was told and then attempted to speak.

"Suffering Succotash…" I burst out laughing at the squeaky voice that emanated. The walk home was a long, slow and friendship healing one. We stopped often and laughed continually.

I never understood how he managed to fool me into his 'grand plans,' time after time. Looking back, I suppose it was mainly because I was the stupid naive one, and Stew was completely mad one. I was his version of my doll, Edward, he manipulated me just as I controlled my doll ... well, I say that ... but he never managed to put his hand up my backside!!!

PLEASE RELEASE HIM

It was a bright, short shirt sleeve sort of day, there was an azure blue sky filled with my favourite type of clouds, the ones that look like giant cotton wool balls, each as white as snow and all racing above you towards the not too distant Pennines as if they were on skateboards. The air was fresh and summer was knocking on the door.

We are in Douglas Street in Moston and two boys are sat on a garden wall, facing each other, legs straddling either side of the brickwork, taking it in turns to dig into a single packet of salt and vinegar crisps, a large bottle of pop sat in between them. A lady walks towards them, a smile appears as she reaches them.

"Have you seen our David, Brian?" It was Kath Marsden, mother of the Marsden clan and daughter of my next door neighbour, Flo.

We both looked up and around, then at each other, fear entered Stews eyes.

"He's in our back garden Kath, erm … we've been playing farmers. I'll just go and get him for you." but before I was able to finish the sentence she was through our gate, and halfway down the path, Kath was nothing if not fleet of foot.

"It's fine, Brian, I'll pop round and get him, his dinner's ready. Is your mum in?" she asked over her shoulder.

"Er...no … she's gone to town with me nana..." I was struggling to get my legs garden side without disturbing our little picnic. I needed to get ahead of her, but the bottle of pop was in the way.

"Move the bottle, Stew, quick...!" Stew grabbed the bottle and pulled it quickly to his chest.

Kath was already down the side of our house when I eventually caught her up, it was a moment later then she saw what playing farmers with Stew and Hammy had meant for her son.

Dave was only five or six years old and he had been hog tied to my mums washing line pole. He stood vertically, with his arms outstretched up at shoulder level, a long broom handle had been shoved through both his jumper sleeves across his small back. His hands were hanging loose out of the cuffs. The brush head was still attached and was by his left hand. On his head was a yellow hat, big and floppy, that I had found in my mother's wardrobe. We had stuffed clumps of grass between the rim and his head. And there he was, tied at his sandaled feet and waist, happy as a sand boy.

"What in heaven's name..." Kath exclaimed, a hand coming to her mouth.

"He's playing at being our scarecrow!" I explained.

"He's bloody tied up, undo him now." I moved from behind her, looking back for help but Stew had evaporated.

"Awwww, but mum, I'm a scarecrow...I'm scaring the birds away for the farmers." Dave insisted in little bird like voice.

"Look at his sleeves and head, he's got grass all over him, there'll be bugs and everything crawling all over him ... for goodness sakes, Brian."

"I know Kath, but, that's what scarecrows are supposed to look like ... the crows might not have been scared otherwise. And to be honest, it might have been Dave's idea, if I think back." I was not finding it easy undoing Dave's bondage and coming up with excuses at the same time. It didn't help Stew had read a book on knots ... and if I'm honest we were really lucky she hadn't called round an hour earlier when he had been showing me an example of the hangman's noose on Dave's tiny, fragile neck.

"I'm just playing with Stew and Bri, mum. If you undo me all the birds will be able to get to all the seeds that the farmers have put in the ground." he complained as his legs were finally freed.

"Bloody farmers!! Your dinners going cold on the dining table ... pull that brush out of his arms, Brian, and where's that Stewart gone? I suppose this was all his idea?" she rambled on irately as she tried to free her little golden haired son.

"I'm not sure! It might have been Dave. Stew had wanted to play kidnappers and tie Dave up in the boot of Brett Dalton's old car in the back entry. Then we were going to pretend to be being chased by the cops, but Dave didn't like having a pillow case over his head while he was all tied up as well ... plus ... we couldn't get Brett's boot open!"

"You, my little boy..." she bent down looking into the face of her newly freed son, "...can play with your sisters from now on, and stay away from that Stewart Neale ... and you should too, Brian," then as is if to emphasise her words she turned to face me, "he's really not a full shilling if you ask me."

Dave was liberated from his yellow headgear, Kath removed it from his head and passed it me.

I looked at her, crestfallen, chastened but nowhere near as disappointed as David. He was near to tears. He had loved his role as a scarecrow, in fact it was several months until I spotted any wildlife at all in our back garden again ... he had proved to be an exceptional example of crow scaring ... screaming and shouting at anything with wings. He almost certainly missed his way in later life ... it was a vocation lost.

"HEY!!! NOOOOO ... I'm not playing with my sisters. Mum, they treat me like a baby, they play girls games like skipping and two-ball..." Kath was dragging a still complaining blonde haired child down our side ginnel..."..."daft, silly songs ... singing one, two, three, O'Leary while you're bouncing balls against the wall..." he looked back at me like a boy off to the electric chair. But there was nothing I could possibly do for him, a mother's love is an invincible force of nature, he would just have to do his time at his sisters pretend tea parties ... like it, or lump it!

I followed them at a safe distance, his unisex red sandals skidding and bungling over the pavement slabs as he failed in his tug of war with his mother. He tried playing dead, dangling like my ventriloquist doll, limbs loose and lifeless but Kath was obviously as strong of arm as she was of mind, she never lost a step. I stood on tip toes to see his final moments before being lifted over the threshold of number 9, three doors down. Then as their door closed shut a head suddenly popped over the wall adjacent to me.

"She gone?" a loud whisper and darting eyes to go with the head.

"Oh, hello Stewart ... you decided to show up now?" I asked sarcastically.

"Didn't see any reason both of us should get another ear bashing. I've had one already this morning off me mam."

"Well, there's a surprise. So have I ... and it's odds on I'll get another later when Kath grasses me up!"

Stew clambered over the wall like a gecko, he then dropped to the floor elegantly. He had this feline quality about him when it came to climbing, an alley cat mind, not a pedigree! No structure fazed him, no height gave him second thoughts.

"What should we do now?" he asked.

"Should I get my ball … we can have a game of wall-ee?" I suggested.

"Or keepy-uppy?" Stew proffered.

"Yeah, I'll go and get my ball..." I turned to go in our front door, then stopped, spun round again, "Kath said Dave's got to play with Paula and Debbie from now on..." I smiled, but I attempted pity at the same time...

"Ha ha … skipping and hopscotch and worst of all their stupid garden picnics … pretend tea parties. Poor ol' Dave." he laughed heartily at the very thought of it.

"I know. He's going to be an expert two-baller too, plainsy's...uppsy's...undersy's...oversy's, and a different song to learn with each one! What's that one where they put a ball in their mum's tights and skip over it?

"Think it's called French skipping … Dave'll look great doing that! He may well end up wearing a skirt...ha ha."

"I'm sure he'd rather be a goal post for us, or that one we played the other day … with the bow and arrow. He was our moving target!" I started giggling, remembering him running along the length of the Church Chapel wall, his little legs a blur and ne'er a complaint or whine as the rubber-suckered arrows continuously bounced off his head.

"Yeah, we called it the Golden Headed Shot … Bernie the bolt … run Dave … faster...ha ha."

"Funny...he he...I'll go and get the ball." I opened up the front door and disappeared inside, still laughing to myself, poor Dave, not allowed to have any real fun with us, at the moment he was probably be the unhappiest boy in Moston!

Mothers!!!! Who'd have 'em?

THE ROADKILL CAFE

"Hi Joe, what's cooking?" I called out over the empty counter.

Me and Stew had taken a break from trying to rediscover the Roman Fort in Broadhurst Park and decamped to the Broadhurst Fields Cafe. All the chairs and tables were empty and we waited patiently at the counter while Marc Bolan sang about Deborah on the radio. A large built man, about 45 years old, with a couple of days growth of beard and several years growth of belly, appeared through the hanging beaded tassels that attempted to stop flies invading his kitchen in this warm weather. His dark hair appeared to have been styled with lard, it was lank and very greasy and flopped onto his forehead on a regular basis. His moustache was thin and barely worth the effort and it was a different colour to the hair on his head … it was ginger … weird!

"Boys…." he took a breath as he wiped his hands on an apron that looked like it was on loan from the local pathologist, dark blood stains were smeared unhealthily all across it.

"...are you hungry?" he finally asked.

"Starvin' Marvin!" I said without looking at him, I was too busy perusing the food on the hand written menu.

"Not so much now!" Stew said under his breath as he stared at his apron.

"Good, I've got some lovely fresh burgers on today. All home made too"

"Are they the same as last weeks? They were brill" I inquired.

"I've tweaked the recipe a little, I've got the Thumper burger on today, and it's lovely and succulent. And only 25p!" he grinned with pride.

"Thumper burger, sounds cool to me." I said licking my lips.

"What else is on the menu, Joe?" Stew asked unable to get a look in while it was in my hands.

"Well, I've just been preparing a Peter Cottontail Mixed Grill or you could try the Harvey Hotdog. Now that's real lush with some ketchup on it." he put his hands on the counter and stared down at us like a judge on Crown Court.

"I'll have the Thumper Burger please." I dropped five 5p's on his counter, letting them bounce, Joe eye's darting with worry that they would fall to the floor. I dug back in my pocket and found another 10p.

"An' give us a Coke, Joe, loads of ice, please." I turned and found a seat, it squealed like fingernails on a chalkboard as I pulled it out leaving Stewart the counter to choose his snack.

"Everything is rabbit, 'init Joe?" Stew said quietly, all them names, they're just all famous rabbits.

"I beg your pardon? All my meat is fresh and locally sourced, I'll have you know!" he shook his head in disgust.

"Yeah, locally sourced off the playing fields over there." Stew pointed across at the Broadhurst Fields football pitches, there was a football match taking place on every pitch, a selection of different coloured football shirts moved around at different speeds, all chasing footballs in a mad frenzy. The field ran for half a mile down to the cemetery wall, bordered by Lightbowne Road and Moston Lane on either side and all this was just forty feet from his front door.

"But, it is all rabbit, isn't it? You're shooting 'em at dawn, aren't you?" Stew accused the cafe owner. Joe brought himself down to his 11 year old accusers face and said in a slightly threatening tone.

"Listen smarty-pants, you find a burger at these prices anywhere else in Manchester and I'll give you a Crackerjack pencil. Does it really matter if the meat has come off a cow or off Hartley Hare?"

"Nope, not to me, I would just like to come out shooting with you that's all." Stew said without flinching in the fat, sweaty face of the head chef. Although his breath nearly knocked him backwards.

"Oh, well." Joe's defenses were lowered now, he pulled himself back to his full height and smiled genially "It'll have to be next Saturday now, the fridge is right full."

"Saturday's great, but I'm not just going to be your red setter fetching your kills ... I want to do some carnage too." Stew shouldered an invisible rifle and closed one eye before 'popping' off two shots.

"No worries, you can borrow my other gun. We'll make a killing … literally!" he laughed. "So what do you fancy?"

"Coke, and toast please. No ice."

"Is that it?" he asked with disappointment.

"Yeah, I don't mind killing the buggers, but I really don't fancy eating 'em. Let's me see if Hammy survives his bunny burger before I take any chances with your cooking."

"Listen, the Mrs. Tiggy Winkle special is to die for." he whispered as if this was only for his significant customers.

"Mrs. Tiggy Winkle? Hedgehog? Really?" Stew squirmed.

"Its fine, the trick is to cook it in clay very slowly over several hours. I've had it on 50 degrees since ten last night. It'll fall right off the bone. The gypsy's love 'em."

"I'll probably fall off my flaming perch if I ate that!" Stew exclaimed.

"Perch? Funny you should say that … I've got some nice carp out of the Clough lake if its fish you are after." he placed both hands on his voluminous hips.

"Joe, Coke and toast, that's it." Stew insisted.

"Well, you don't know what you are missing." he turned slowly, not unlike a bull elephant in a telephone box, parted the plastic tassels then disappeared back into the kitchen.

"Oh I think I do! Botulism for starters!!" Stew said before he joined me at the table.

"Sorted?" I asked knife and fork in my hand and banging gently on the table top.

"Sorted. Toast."

"I can't, I ain't got me Coke yet."

"Not toast." he raised an empty hand, "Toast!" he bit into an imaginary piece of grilled bread in explanation.

"Ahh, thought you meant… "I raised my empty hand in the air and didn't bother finishing my sentence as Stew was shaking his head.

He leaned back in his chair and crossed his legs, his eyes started to follow two flies that buzzed quietly across the room from the big window to the light bulb and returning again and again in an endless relay.

"I really don't why we bother coming to eat here, I honestly think we are the only people who ever do." he spat out.

"It's cheap and don't forget he has his special burgers on every week, like last week's burger with a side order of guacamole."

"Guacamole is green, Hammy. Joe's version was bright red … I suspect that was 'guaca-mole'!

"It was very meaty, I admit." I grimaced slightly. "If it wasn't 'have-a-ca-doo', what do you think it was?"

"Have-a-ca-doo? Do you mean avocado?" Stew asked sarcastically.

"It's spelt have-a-ca-doo!"

"Yet it's pronounced avocado, idiot!"

The curtains swished and Joe emerged holding two plates, one with a big burger on it and another with two slices of well toasted pieces of bread. Golden, melting butter spilling off the toast onto the small, cracked plate. On his feet I noticed he had big furry, grey slippers on. He smiled with pride as he noticed us looking down.

"Do you like 'em? Made 'em meself. Real fur slippers ... they'd cost a bomb in Kendal's, these would!"

"You don't waste a bit of the poor things, do you, Joe?" Stew laughed.

"Of course not, you should see my bedspread!"

"I'd rather just have my food, please."

"Of course. Toast...?" he placed it down in front of Stew. "... and a Thumper burger. Do you want any relish with that, Hammy?" he asked me.

"Oooh, have you got some of that yellow stuff?"

"Mustard?" he scratched his mucky fingers through his oily hair.

"Noooo, Piccadilly!"

"Yep, give me a second." he leaned over the counter slowly revealing a butt crack you could have parked the front wheel of a Harley Davidson in. Stew took a large bite of his toast and smiled.

"Have you noticed that all the food in here is named after animals, not too obviously like, but if you just think about it." he whispered, nodding at my plate.

"What? You mean it's not proper food? So ... is yours stoat?" I blabbered out.

"Stoat? I've got toast!" he lifted the bread to his mouth and took a bite, butter dripping down onto his lime green tee-shirt.

"Yeah, but it's an 'anagran' of stoat, init?"

Stew stopped chewing and opened his mouth, his tongue slowly came out to its full extent, on it was sat a well masticated ball of toast. He raised the plate to his mouth with both hands and let it roll back on to it.

"Cokes, boys." he was at our side again, he was exceptionally light on his feet for a man of over twenty stone.

"What's wrong with your toast? He asked accusingly of Stew.

"What's it made of?" he pointed at the bread.

"It's just bread, toasted." he said a little bit lost at the question.

"So, it's not an animal then?" Stewart was now staring up at the giant chef.

"Animal? It's Rathbones. I only had it delivered fresh this morning.

"Rat-bones!! Flaming Nora, that's gotta be illegal, man!" Stew screamed out, he took an enormous glug of Coke and gargled, raced to the door and spat all over his step. "Come on Hammy, we are out of here."

I picked up my burger and pushed back my chair with a high pitched scraping of chair leg on the poorly varnished wood.

"Sorry, Joe, we're off." I gave him my best Stan Laurel smile, he shrugged.

"Don't forget your free 'lucky' rabbits foot." he pulled a small grey, hairy claw from his Levi's and handed it to me.

"I've always wanted one of these." I stroked it and showed it off to Stew at the door. "It's a lucky rabbit's foot!" I explained.

88

"Yeah, but unlucky flippin' rabbit! One minute."
Stew stuck his head back in the shop. "Joe … Saturday
morning? What time does the bloodshed start?"

Joe stared at him for a second before
understanding the question.

"Oh, the rabbit hunt? Get here for 5 a.m. They'll
be sat waiting for us." he smiled an evil grin … Stew
smiled back one darker and more malevolent and said in
his best Elmer Fudd voice.

"I hate wittle gway wabbits!" he laughed out
loud at his own joke.

"Just don't be late or you'll miss the fun."

"Don't worry, I wouldn't miss it for the world."

"Come on Stew, let's go and watch some
togger." I called from the kerb.

"Coming, just sorting out a mass murder."

"Some things never change, do they Stew?" I
laughed as I legged it across the empty road.

"I'm just a boy who can't say no … to
annihilation!"

HANNIBAL CRACKERS

We were walking up Brendon Avenue, the sun was dropping slowly as the early evening started its journey en route to dusk. Inside my grey shorts my grubby fingers were juggling a 'lucky' stone in one pocket and a 134'er conker in the other. My shorter, thinner, hairier and vainer friend was busy sliding his aluminium through his shiny, centre-parted hair for about the 900th time that day.

"Did you go to the circus last night?" I asked my closest friend and yet severest critic.

"Nah, circuses are rubbish." another sweeping statement from the mouth of the oracle.

"Rubbish? They ain't rubbish, are they? They've got lions and tigers in 'em and clowns!"

"Clowns freak me out, all that make up on men, it's like they are hiding something!" he shivered as we turned down the ginnel at the side of Scotty's house.

"There's actually a name for the fear of clowns."

"Is there?"

"Yeah. Chicken!" I burst out laughing.

"Chicken? Really … me? The boy who put two ferret down my shorts … for ten minutes!

"So why are you so down on clowns?"

"I don't trust 'em! They're either frowning with tears painted on their face or smiling this crazy, big red lipped grin that makes you think they are about to chop your head off!"

"Stew, they're funny, broken cars, tiny bikes and buckets of confetti...he he." I giggled at the thought of their japes.

"That's ain't funny. Candid Camera, now that's funny!"

"Oh, I love that, Jonathan Routh is the funniest man alive!" a sharp right along Scotty's back fence and we were approaching the start of the Diggy. Stew stopped to pontificate.

"See, a man sticking his head out of a manhole cover and asking if this is Euston Underground station, now that's funny or asking a man to check his oil while he goes to the loo ... and they've took the engine out of the car and just rolled it down a hill onto the petrol station forecourt leaving the guy scratching his head when he can't find motor under the bonnet ... FUNNY!"

"Yeah, but..."

"No buts Hammy, if a clown asked you to do that you'd think ... check your own flipping oil, freak!" he began walking again.

"God, you really don't like clowns, do you?"

"They are evil, twisted people. They are unhappy people in real life and too many are dwarfs ... freaks!"

"Really though, there is a name for it ... like arachnophobia."

"That's the fear of anoraks, not clowns!" he said as he took the lead on a foot worn path running down the back of the houses on Brendon Avenue.

91

Ten yards onto the path and Stew stopped and cocked his head to one side.

"What?" alarm bells began ringing in my head.

"Shhh!" Stew raised his arm to quieten me.

There, I heard it now. An indistinct but definite noise to our left, it was the sound of something heavy rolling over ... then the very loud sound of something exhaling.

"What the Fuehrer...! Stew cried and jumped back from the high, dry grass that reached up to his sunken chest.

"Let's run!" I tried to grab my friend.

"No. Wait, we'll have to investigate."

"Why?" It might be a dragon!

"Shush, idiot!" he put a finger to his mouth.

"What you doing?" I asked. He was slowly, but surely, entering the unknown. Each step caused a rustle and soft crunch as the grass stems were crushed down by his weight.

"Are you mad?" I had both hands in my hair now. "Oh, forget that question, but if you get eaten, it'll be your own fault because don't think I will be fighting any dragon to get you out of its mouth!" I insisted.

Suddenly, about six foot ahead of Stew out of the grass a large, dark grey tube of wrinkles came rising out of the grass.

"Watch out Stew, it's a giant anaconda!" I squealed.

"No it's not." he stepped back while still trying to peer over the grass.

"Let's get out of here." I turned and started running back towards the ginnel exit.

"Hammy ... stop, it's not a snake." Stew shouted after me.

I slowed and cautiously turned back towards him, hands caressing my hair still.

"What is it then?"

"It's an elephant!" as he said this there was a trumpet call and from the depths of the grass a baby elephant appeared, struggling to its feet.

"Oh...my...god!" I said under my breath

"Oh...mein...kampf!" Stew shouted as he bounced like Tigger up and down. "I saw him first ... he's mine!" he had shouted out so I wouldn't get a 'bags' on it.

"It's an elephant! What you going to do with an elephant?"

"Anything I want, nobody's going to stop me now!" he giggled and carefully approached the now standing beast. Stew's head was at eye level to it and as he got close its trunk rose and touched his already ruffled hair.

"He likes me, Hammy, he only flipping like me! Hello...erm...I'm gonna call you Panzer, hello Panzer!"

"You really need to cut back on this German fixation, Stew!" I told him as I bravely approached them.

"Look at him ... he's only a baby." he was stroking the animals head.

"Careful, it might...erm...bite?"

"They don't bite, Dumbo ... ha ha ... Dumbo! Geddit?" he still gazed adoringly into his new pets eyes as he giggled at his own gag.

"Well, he might well strangle you." I theorised.

"No he won't, he loves me! Don't you?" Stew grabbed one of the slow flapping ears and turned it slowly, he pulled and 'Panzer' followed him.

"Where you going?" I said in a panicked tone.

"He needs to eat, they eat leaves and there's load of leaves on these privets." ahead of Stew was thirty foot or more of large, out of control privet hedging. When they reached them, Stew encouraged it to grab the branches with its trunk. Slowly but surely it enveloped then stripped a branch, folding the end of its trunk to grasp the leaves he then forced them into its open mouth.

"Flaming 'eck, its doing it!" I said in disbelief.

"I know, it'll do anything I tell it now. I'm like that boy and the lion." he nodded at me, still holding the baby elephants left ear.

"The one who had his fingers bit off at Belle Vue?"

"No, idiot! The one they were talking about in Sunday school ... the boy pulled the nail out of the lions bum, then the lion loved him and they went round together killing everyone.

"Daniel? He wasn't a mass murderer!"

"Are you sure? Didn't he make the lion rip people's throats out, everyone was scared of them, sure that's what happened."

"No, he was a Christian!"

"So was Hitler!" Stew had let go of the ear now and was facing me now as the animal decimated the foliage.

"Yeah, but … ooooh Stew, watch out!!!"

"What? Is someone coming?" he started to duck out of sight into the deep grass.

"No, the elephants starting to lift it's…" but my warning was too late, Panzer had already done a large dump right on Stews feet.

"Oh shiesse!" he cried out as he stared at the mess covering his feet.

"That's about right, it is shiesse!" I had got within touching range of Panzer now. "What we gonna do with an elephant?"

"What do you mean?" Stew asked as he shook one foot then the other in an attempt to clear the dung from his feet.

"Should we go to the police?"

"Are you out of your tiny mind?" he forgot about the defecation that was attached to his shoes, socks and shins. "Give him up! He's probably run away from that circus, and if he has it's because he ain't happy!"

"But we can't keep him, he is proper maffis!"

"I've got an idea!"

"I am not robbing any banks!" I insisted.

"Actually that hadn't crossed my mind, but…" he bit his bottom lip and his eyes disappeared high into his head.

"Stew...Stew...concentrate."

"What, oh yeah, we can leave the looting and plundering until later, we need to get him hidden, and fast."

"Hide him? Where in one of our back yards?"

"No, in the Clough, It's the perfect place!" he said proudly.

"Boggart Hole Clough?" I looked at him as if he's lost any sense of reality.

"It's the nearest thing we've got to Africa in Moston!"

"How in heavens name are we getting him up Kenyon Lane without some noticing we have a three ton elephant walking between us? We can't just throw a blanket over him, can we?"

"No … you're right. We will have to sneak out of our beds at one o'clock and we take him up then!"

"And we just hope no one see's him, hears him or he decides to go for a walk away from here!"

"No, we are going to have to hide him!" he leaned against the beast and scratched his head.

"Oh good, that's simple then. Should I dig a really big hole?" I asked sarcastically.

"Yeah … then put yourself in it, idiot boy! No, I'll break into Billy Owens garage, we can hide him in there for now."

"But he's got that mad dog in there!"

"I've got an elephant, and an elephant trumps any dog in the world ... every day of the week! Come on." he grabbed Panzer by the ear and pulled him along through the grass, the elephant's small eye looking deeply at me as we went.

"They don't eat meat, now you're sure of that aren't you?" keeping just far enough away so his trunk couldn't make a grab for me.

"No, stop panicking, empty head."

Stew persuaded me to hold on to Panzers leathery ear while he used a large metal bar to jemmy the lock off the door of Billy Owens garage door. While Stew banged and manipulated the lock away from the woodwork, inside a large alsatian dog was going berserk, ready to defend his 'manor'. The padlock creaked then suddenly popped from one side of the large wooden gates.

"Right, pull Panzer over here." Stew pointed to a central point directly in front of the gates, facing the barking.

Stew placed himself to one side of a gate and pulled it wide open, the ill-fitting, rotting gate scraped the dirt at the base as he did. Out bounded a snarling dog, teeth bared and preparing for bloodshed ... it skidded to an immediate halt in front of our planet's largest animal, it took a moment for its head to rise high enough to make eye contact ... Panzer seemed to smile as he raised its trunk, the bellow that emanated out of that elevated trunk vibrated against my chest and weakened my bladder slightly.

The Alsatian stuck its tail halfway up its backside and did a sharp right hand turn before disappearing into the gloom across the Diggy ... never to be seen again.

"See ... trumped him!" Stew smiled at me.

"Cripes, I think you 'trunked' him!" I shook my head as I tried to clear the ringing noise from within, it was like early onset tinnitus.

"Come on Panzer, in you come." Stew called to him, I pulled gently on his ear and he began walking into the dark bowels of our local rag and bone man's holding house. There was a long table down the middle with a selection of collected clothes that were halfway through of being sorted into one sort of category or another.

Panzer decided the bucket of water just inside the door needed drinking and he dunked his trunk deep into the liquid and slurped half immediately up into his trunk.

"Woooah, he's not gonna squirt us is he?" I backed outside again.

"No, watch." Stew said without fear. Panzer jammed his trunk in his mouth and with a good blow of his nose emptied the water down his throat.

"What now?"

"Get him over here when he's finished the water." Stew stood over an enormous pile of rags. "He can kip on here."

Once our elephant drank the bucket dry and we had coaxed him to lay amongst the clothes, Stew found some rope and tied one end round his front leg and the other end to a large, central supporting pole that kept the roof from falling down.

"Can't have him wandering off, can we?"

"Can we go home now? It's getting late." I said.

We bade farewell to young friend and raced home. My head was full of doubt and worry, Stews head was full of the thoughts of World domination.

I'd never had problems sleeping and so it was that night ... I was snoring away like a potbellied pig. My dream was vivid, I was an eagle and I was chomping down on ice cream clouds! My lovely calm dreams were rudely interrupted by the banging of gunshots from the ground where giant bears fired up at me as I flew through my edible clouds. A really loud bang made my eyelids burst open ... there I lay in the dark, my feather filled pillow in my mouth and the constant rattle of stones on my bedroom window.

I spat out the pillow and knelt up at the window, pulled the curtain to one side, tentatively. I looked out, worried the 'bogey' man would be there ready to chew my head off ... but it was worse!! It was Stew, smiling maniacally from the roof of our outside loo. In the dark of the night his choppers were lit up like a beacon, his face was smeared with black stripes. He waved a welcome and mouthed the words 'come on!'

Reluctantly I swept my sheets back and bent down feeling around on the floor for my clothes. Five minutes later I was picking my way down the stairs slowly ... each step took fifteen seconds ... each step was as if I was walking through a minefield, praying it wouldn't creak. Several lifetimes later I reached the bottom and stepped onto cold lino in the kitchen. Unbolting the back door was a case of swiveling the bolt as I slid it across with my left hand and lifted the latch with my right. The door was inched open until I was able to squeeze my tubby, young body through into the night air then pull it slowly, shut behind me.

"Hey, are you excited?" Stew whispered in a giggly voice.

"No, me mum and dad will kill me if they ever find out. It's flipping freezing, my nipples are pointing out like drawing pins!" I said as I rubbed at my little man boobs.

"Hammy, I really didn't need to know that! Come on, let's go and get Panzer to the park."

We exited the yard and jogged slowly up Rudd Street under the orange street lights, our shadows dancing around us as we ran. We were on the Diggy within two minutes and at Billy's garage door a minute later with Stew inspecting the large, black gate for the signs of any tampering.

"The doors still tied up." he gave me the thumbs up and pulled an enormous curved knife from his belt.

"What the hell is that?" I cried out.

"It's a kukri! The gurkhas use them to cut people's ears off! I swapped it for one of my dad's expensive watches"

"Who did you swap it with?"

"A copper. He'd taken it off a United fan at the match!"

"What, then he just stopped you and asked if you wanted it?"

"No, he threatened to cut off my 'billy's' with it when he caught me shoving a dog turd up his police car exhaust!"

"What, then he just offered it you?

"Nooooo ... for God's sake man! I just admired it, blah di blah ... and before you know it, I've scraped the turd from his exhaust and gone home to 'borrow' me dads watch and voila!!!" he held up the deadly weapon and flashed it through the air theatrically.

"You've just got to love a British cop! Hey, we're not going to be chopping off anyone's ears are we?"

"I hope not, but better safe than sorry, hey?" he smiled and started sawing at the string.

"I really can't see any scenario where we need to hack off any ears, can you?"

"Look..." he brought the knife up close to my right cheek. "...it's great for chopping bamboo, hacking at branches, killing animals of all sizes ... Hammy, it's the perfect instrument for jungle survival ... and that's where we are going, Boggart Hole Clough, the jungle!" he turned and concentrated on finishing his cutting. "..Have you brought anything for our perilous expedition?"

"A peanut butter sandwich!"

"A peanut butter butty...!" utter disbelief in his voice.

"It's got strawberry jam on it just like the Americans do it!"

"It always comes down to me, doesn't it? Good job I've brought this," he held up the knife, "this..." he opened his jacket on the right side so I could see a homemade catapult, "...and look at this!" he pulled the left side open and stuck in his trousers was a gun.

"A GUN!"

"It's not real yet!" he pulled it out. "It's a copy of the most powerful handgun in the world, .44 Magnum." He pointed it at my head and pretended to shoot, doing the recoil as he went…"BOOOOOM!" he shoved it back in his belt and smiled.

"But what good is it if it doesn't fire?"

"It'll still guaranteed to make someone pooh their kecks!" he laughed then continued. "Our Caroline hasn't slept properly for three weeks since I tied her to the washing line pole and pretended she was on the end of gangland assassination.

I took a bite out of my sandwich and felt like a Shanghaied sailor. Taken from a comfortable, warm bed by a crazy pirate and to forced sail the seven seas of mayhem.

The door lurched open slowly and Stew pulled a small torch from his pocket, he was like a human Swiss knife, he shone it inside and eventually landed the light on our grey beast.

"Come on, don't scare him." said the boy with the curved cutlass, handgun and catapult to the boy with a potentially stomach filling peanut butter sandwich!

Stew approached, the elephant stirred, focused on the little boy by his head and began to struggle to its feet, as it did Stew leaned in and placed his hand on his head and stroked him in long, soft movements. Panzer used his trunk to sniff and touch Stews short, wiry body.

"Here…" he turned and shone the torch in my eyes as he walked back towards me. The blindness was intentional, while I struggled to see he grabbed my thick, heavily laden sandwich.

"What you doing" I lunged into the darkness in search of the food, but before my eyesight was restored he was already placing it in the trunk of our friend. It was consumed in seconds, the trunk searched out more nourishment but only found disappointment.

"Hey, I was eating that!" I stood, hands by my side rigid with anger and a little hunger.

"Was eating it ... it's gone, get over it, you're really not going to starve, are you?"

I pulled my face pointlessly, it was too dark for Stew to see my rage. He just untied the knot from round Panzers neck and tugged on his ear, he began to move, his head down and its tree trunk legs started thumping into the ground and like three desperadoes we exited the garage and moved slowly back out into the fresh, cool night air. One baby elephant, flanked by two young boys ... it was ironic really ... I'd read about boys running away to join the circus ... not so may books on boys running away from the circus!

"I think it might be easier if I rode him!" Stew declared from the other side of Panzers head.

"What, like a horse?" I shouted back.

"No, like an elephant. I'll sit on his neck, like Sabu!"

"Sabu?" had I heard right?

"Elephant Boy! He's an actor, a dead old one." he explained.

"Elephant Boy?"

"Get your dad to tell you about him. Stop so I can climb aboard."

"How you getting up there?"

"If I tap its leg, it'll probably lift it up so I can stand on it and get on." Stew leant down and grabbed a small stick off the floor near his foot. He gently tapped the elephant on the knee.

"Woooooah!" I cried out … Panzer appeared to be attempting a forward roll.

"Bloody Nora!" Stew screamed as he leapt back as Panzer did a handstand, his large rear legs pointing up at the moon.

"I thought he was going to lift his knee!"

"Well, that's what they did on Billy Smart's Circus on telly. I didn't think he'd stand on his head!"

The elephant slowly returned to earth with a bump.

"Well at least we know he can do tricks! It might be easier if you just give me a boost up, then I'll just climb on him." I reluctantly dovetailed my fingers on both hands and with a quick upward thrust I launched Stew onto the back of the baby elephant, he then swung his left leg over and slid into the small depression between neck and body.

"Yeehaaahhh! Okay Panzer, it's only me, right, let's try this." he gently tapped his heels on the front shoulders of Panzer and called quietly. "Gee up." the elephant lumbered forward slowly.

"Oh my god, you're riding an elephant."

"I'm an elephant boy, ha ha."

After just a few minutes, Stew had worked out the steering. Basically it was holding the top of Panzers ears and pulling hard on the left ear to turn left … or the

104

right one to go the other way. We finally began our march across the Diggy, round the back of the Sharon Church and down an empty McConnell Road onto the deserted Kenyon Lane. Stew's bravado occasionally made him try to accelerate but his fledgling genitalia struggled with the bouncing up and down on the elephant's tough hide and even harder skull. He decided on a gentle plodding would suffice.

"What we doing with him when we get to the Clough? Just letting him go?"

"No, we can't just slap his butt and go home ... I thought we could take him to the island. He can live there, safe from the cruel circus people."

"We don't really know they're cruel, do we?" I asked.

"They must be, why else has he run away? It's just lucky he met us ... we are freedom fighters now. In future we can raid zoos and free lions, tigers, crocodiles and chimps, we can bring them to the Clough! They can all live on the island together, all safe." he smiled and patted his elephantine transportation on the head. "Can't we, boy?"

"Safe? What about the family's just out for a walk on Sundays and their young lad getting eaten by enormous wild cat? What about the boaters rowing round the island suddenly having a croc bite their boat in two then being chomped to death?"

Stew puffed his cheeks out.

"Why do you always look on the black side of everything? You really are a misery guts, the animals will be happy and in the future there'll be opportunities for big game hunting, here…" he swirled his hands out wide, his kukri in one hand his elephant stick in the other, "… in North Manchester, brilliant!" he sat up tall on the back of his new mate and tapped him again with the stick.

"Onward Panzer," he cried out. "freedom is just around the corner!" we crossed Moston Lane and headed down passed the Museum towards the Clough entrance.

Worsley Avenue at two thirty in the morning seems so much longer than I ever remember it being in daylight. Now that may have been the fear of the dark playing on my mind or the thought of my father unbuckling his belt and slapping it on a large, strong, open palm. In reality, I think the fact that we had, in essence, stolen a baby African elephant from a touring circus and we were only minutes away from actually being off Mostons main thoroughfares and yet to be spotted. We never, ever got lucky. We were bound to be caught.

My mind kept flitting to a scenario us both stood in the dock. Stew, his hair the only visible part of him whereas I would be tall enough to face a thousand people in the gallery. Clowns, trapeze artists and women with beards would all be hissing as each charge was read out. I'd be swearing on the Bible to tell the truth, the whole truth … Stew insisting he would say anything unless he could swear on Hitler's, Mein Kampf!!

"Hey Lurch!" my overactive mind swiftly returned to the cold avenue.

"What?" I looked up at Stew, bobbing with each of the elephants steps.

"Not far now, I can see the entrance to the Clough."

"There's no lights in there, it'll be pitch black … and we have to cross the bridge where they say the 'White Lady' walks!"

"I know, how exciting is that?"

"Exciting!! She'll have her head in her hands, what if I have a heart attack if I see her!" I mumbled in fear.

"That'd be funny, then you could be the 'White Boy!' A ghost I knew personally … how cool would that be?" he said as he gazed into his euphoric horizon of wild animals and ghostly best mates.

"Not that much, if I'm honest! It's not how I had seen my future … a professional haunter!" I said grimly.

"I could rent you out to castles and stately homes. Bet you'd get loads of money for doing that."

"So I'm dead and now I've become the property of you? What if I just fancy going to heaven, you know, sit on a cloud with a harp and get my wings … the stuff normal people want to do when they pop their clogs."

"Heaven? Yeah, good luck with that one!" he burst out laughing as he continued to bobbed up and down above my head.

"Hey, I'm a good boy!" I stopped and stared at him. "...it's you that won't get through the 'Pearly Gates'..." I jogged to catch them up again, "...I am going to heaven, and you know it. I don't swear, smoke or steal..." I stopped. Had I stole an elephant? Nah, Stew had nicked it, I was only here to make sure he didn't kill it or himself ... I was God's care in the community worker!

"Methinks you protest too much." he called back to me.

In my head I said the Lord's Prayer ... emphasising the 'deliverance from Evil!' I'll be okay, anyway I wasn't planning on dying anytime soon, so there would be plenty of time to do good 'stuff'. There was bob a job, tidying my room and putting my undies in the dirty washing. Yep, heaven was still within my grasp.

"Oh bugger!!" Stews voice broke my reverie.

"What?"

"Milky." Stew exclaimed.

Around the corner, just before entering the steep path down into the Clough came a whirring, slow moving, milk float. Heavily laden with hundreds of bottles of milk, each and every one rattling in their crates.

"Oh no, we are one minute from freedom and we are going to be spotted!" Stew said.

I crouched behind the still walking elephant, I decided anonymity was the best policy. I heard the float brake hard ... the crates slide forward and the 'empties' rattle loudly in their berths.

"Morning matey!" Stew called out calmly to the milkman, who sat forward, chest on the steering wheel, face planted on the enormous windscreen and his eyes wide and disbelieving.

"Errr...morning." his reply was wavering and full of self-doubt.

We slowly walked past the front of his vehicle, casting a dark shadow over the man's pale face and entered the dark world of Boggart Hole Clough by night. The last thing the milkman saw was the waggling bottom of an elephant's backside, its tail swishing merrily as it walked.

"They'll find us now. Let's ditch him and do a runner, we can be home and back in bed before it gets out of hand." I pleaded as I walked quickly alongside them.

"Nope, the lakes not far and that milkman might not say anything!"

"Of course he won't! Why should he? He'll probably look at the headline in Manchester Evening News tomorrow … Elephant on the Loose … and he'll just think, it's probably a different elephant!"

"Exactly!" Stew cried out as the hill got steeper down towards the bridge at the 'bottoms' of the Clough. "We are hiding in plain sight!"

"We get him to the island and then get home. You can bring him food on your own…." in the pitch dark I realised I was talking to myself. "Where are you..?" I cried out.

"He's found a crab apple tree … he's stuffing his face." Stew explained somewhere off to my left.

Once he had had his fill we continued down the steep slope and onto the bridge that spanned a deep gorge. I held onto Panzers ear and looked into the darkness for any signs of an apparition.

My heart was beating like it had a wild cat in it, and fighting to get out. I hate the unknown, always have … always will.

We crossed the unhaunted bridge and turned a sharp right. The Clough is a park of valleys, we had come a long way down after entering … now it was time to begin climbing. The hill was a long, winding and arduous climb but we knew when we arrived at the top the Lake would sit just fifty feet to our left. Panzers steps were slower now, Stew, feeling guilty, dismounted and grabbed his other ear.

"Soon be on Elephant Island, matey, and all the swans you can eat!" he said encouragingly.

"I thought you said they are vegetarian, Stew?"

"Starvation can change anyone's diet, Bri!"

"What's that supposed to mean? Do you think he'll eat a swan for breakfast?"

"Definitely, goose, swan, rats and fish … it's just a case of using your environment fully … its how 'devolution works.' Humans were veggies until we found out how good bacon tastes, now we eat everything...the French even eat frogs and snails!"

"Snails!" I felt sick at the very thought.

"Yep, and even worse than that … with garlic!!"

"Flaming hell, the dirty gets!"

"So, swan sounds a lot more tasty than frogs with garlic...urghhh!" he declared.

"Spose, what if he gets a taste for human 'beans'?!"

"It's survival of the fittest, Hammy, life is a fight to the death, a struggle between man and beast … remember, there's always someone trying to plant a machete in your head!"

"Stew?"

"What?"

"What books do you read? 'Cos in Enid Blyton's 'Five Get into a Fix,' they never mention anything like that!"

"Cos that's not real, idiot. That's fantasy ... here, in real life we are liable to be drowned getting across the Lake or at best have leeches sucking blood from our goolies. There might be poachers out there with wild dogs ready to kidnap us and sell us on the white slave trade market!"

"I really love playing out with you. It's never the same with Geoff or Digger, they just want to play football or cricket ... talk about Gilligan's Island or Thunderbirds. You, well, you somehow make life more fun..." I tried really hard to put as much sarcasm into that sentence as possible. It sadly arrived on his eardrums as a lovely big compliment!

"Cheers, Hammy." he thanked me as we reached the summit of the hill, just as the moon finally made an appearance, finding a crack in the clouds. Big and white, like a searchlight, it sat just above the tree line of the island which floated in the middle of the large, dark pool of water that had silver glints of moonlight dancing on the surface, Clough Lake.

"Elephant Island, Hammy, on Freedom Lake!"

"Freedom Lake? More like it'll be loss of Freedom Lake, when they find us!" I said dismally.

"They'll never find us!" the quiet of the night was swiftly shattered by the distant sound of sirens from several emergency vehicles. "...and if they do, they'll never take us alive!" he pulled on Panzers ear and he seemed to trumpet in agreement. Stew then plodded him forward, towards the cold, uninviting pond.

An expanse of water under moonlight can be many things to many people, romantic, poetic, artistic and in certain situations, even enticing … but, if you are eleven years old and teamed up with a slightly dislodged best friend, that water just screams terror at you … especially if it sounds like 93% of North Manchester's 'boys in blue' are descending on you from all angles.

"How, in the name of 'Cheeses Cripes' are we going to get across there?" I asked as we stood on the edge of the black water that denied our passage to the island.

"Well, I'm gonna get back on my mate here." Stew declared.

"Can I get up too?"

"Nah, he's an elephant, not a Brontosaurus!" the laugh he gave, showed fear of any kind hasn't arrived in Stews world.

"Hey, I've lost some weight recently." I said angrily.

"You had your hair cut … that's not a diet!"

"Yeah, funny. Look, you two go over to the island, release one of the rowing boats from its mooring and bring it back for me."

"Now you're thinking, Batman."

"Up here for thinking…" I tapped the side of my head, "…down here for weeing!" I grabbed my crotch.

"Well, I'm not sure that's how the saying goes … I think it's dancing, not peeing." Stew said as he struggled to pull himself up onto Panzers back.

"You can't dance with your willy!" I laughed.

"You tell that to James Brown! Have you seen that guy dance to 'Sex Machine?' "

"No...what's a sex machine?" I wondered out loud.

The sound of sirens were closer now, louder on the White Moss side. They would be coming into the Clough very soon.

"Sex Machine is a..." Stew started before I interrupted.

"It doesn't matter, Stew. Just go and get a boat before we are arrested." Stew nodded and asked for help to clamber aboard our pet.

Panzer tested the water with his trunk then tentatively entered the water, not carefully enough, though. The angle and depth of the lake proved too steep and he went head first into the water with an enormous splash. Stew went flying off his back through the air and disappeared in the gloom.

"Stew … Stew, are you alright?" I called fearing the worst.

For a few seconds I was unable to see anything but the dark silhouette of an elephant and a spraying trunk … then a high pitched squeal cut through the air like a scalpel.

"F..f..f..flaming Nora, Hammy! It's f..f..flipping f..f..freezing!" I could make out a vague image of a boy, stood, hands stuck by his side up to his snake belt in the water.

"You okay?" I called.

"Do I look okay?"

"I can't see, it's too dark!" I explained.

"Well, I'm up to my knackers in ice cold water, I look like a drowned rat! Let's try and guess how I feel!"

"Wet?"

"Course I'm bloody wet, you bleeding idiot! Wet!?" he shouted angrily.

"Should I climb on Panzers back now? You may as well walk across."

"Great!!" he said through the darkness. "Just hurry up, I've just see some lights behind the boat house."

I turned to see several white lights, like mini searchlights sweeping through the inky night sky.

"Here Panzer, come on boy..." I clicked my fingers like I needed a waiter, clicked my tongue like he was a puppy ... surprisingly it worked. He pushed slowly through the water to my side and allowed me to climb onto his neck.

"Oh..my..God!" I said slowly.

"What's wrong now?" Stew's voice asked up ahead.

"I've just split my pants...wide open. My mum is going to kill me!"

"Think in the great scheme of the last six hours, pant splitting is one of the smaller issues when it comes to parental punishment, Hammy!"

"But I've no undies on! My bits are dangling on its head...oooh...and...Arghhh. Every time he takes a step..ooof..they are getting caught in the wrinkles of his neck!"

"No undies!!!? What's that all about? Commando Bri!! har har" he shouted as he splashed towards the island.

"My mum had took my dirty ones downstairs to wash when I went to bed..flipping..'eck..this is gooly murder!"

"Nearly there now" he called.

The island looked darker than I had expected as it loomed large over our heads, there wasn't that feeling of freedom or sanctuary I'd been hoping for. It just felt like we had made our way across to a dead end ... it appeared as if there would be no escape from the long arm of the law!

"You do realise we will be surrounded on here? It's check mate!" I said to Stew as he clambered onto the muddy bank and out of the water. He stood and drained a flood of water from his clothes.

"I'll going to think like Rommel ... we'll counter their pincer movement ... I'll use shock and oar!" he stood, arms on his hips, his head tipped slightly upwards towards the moon, his bottom lip stuck out ... he had a look of Benito Mussolini.

"You're proper potty, really full on, not right!" I declared as I dismounted my ride, pulled off my grey jumper and tied it round my waist to try and hide my shrunken genitalia.

"No, Rommel, he was a genius ... I read about him, some of his war strategies were brilliant, confusing the enemy all the time."

"The enemy? I suppose that was the Allies …
and that was us. My Granddad and yours were the Allies!
You can't call us the enemy!"

"You know what I mean, you awkward get."

"So, this Rommel … he was brilliant? What did
he do?"

"He fought all across North Africa!"

"Didn't we win that?"

"Err … yeah, but only just!" he explained.

"What else did he do?"

"He placed a briefcase at the feet of Hitler, to
blow him up."

"Wouldn't he have been better using a bomb?" I
asked bemused.

"The bomb was in the briefcase! Idiot!" he
exclaimed.

"Ohh … so he killed Hitler?"

"No, it was under a table next to Adolf... (First
name terms!!)...and then he moved. When the bomb went
off it didn't kill him. Burst his eardrums, though."

"Did this Rommel do anything successfully …
apart from giving Hitler earache?"

"When he knew the German police were coming
for him … he committed suicide."

"Brilliant, all of our plans are based on a Nazi. A
rubbish Nazi, at that, who was crap at everything he tried
to do … bar topping himself!!" I grabbed Panzers ear and
enticed him onto the island just as the flashlights reached
the lake.

"It'll be alright as long as we keep quiet, they'll
just go round the island and then go further into the park

when they find nothing. When they've gone we can then row back across the lake and sneak home. We can bring food for Panzer by hiring the boat on a Saturday and Sunday and throwing food to him as we row round."

"I like the idea of going home, getting some fresh 'grundy's' on … my tackle has shrunk down to nowt!"

"Like I said, let's just keep quiet."

It was like Stew's words were a cue for a song, Panzer raised his trunk and trumpeted out a sound old Satchmo would have struggled reach … loud and proud … a split second later eight powerful torches landed on two boys, one was holding his 'knackers' in his right hand, and in between them was a gleeful looking elephant … he trumpeted again.

"Sarge, we've got 'em, they're on the island." the voice of one policeman talking into his radio carried across the water like a scud missile.

"Bugger!" Stew sent a verbal scud back in the opposite direction.

"Boy's, it's time to let us take Mindy home!" a man's voice called from the cluster of lights.

"Mindy? He's a girl?" Stew whispered to me.

"Well, I never looked!" I whispered back, "Does it matter?"

"I would have called her Pansy … not Panzer!" he explained.

"Boy's, are you listening?" the voice again.

"You'll never take us alive, Rozzer!" Stew screamed through the night.

"Stew, I'm not topping myself, I have things to do ... stand on the Stretford End ... watch England win the World Cup in Mexico in a couple of weeks and I need to kiss a girl before I die!"

"You've never kissed a girl!!?"

"No, I'm only 11!"

"You are definitely borderline puff!" he suggested.

"If I was a puff, would I want to kiss a girl?" the logic was on my side.

"But have you tried your mum's clothes on?"

"Have I 'eckers like! Why would I?"

"Okay ... calm down, I was only asking. Blinking heck, think I touched a nerve?"

"Boy's we are going to row across in five minutes, we have to take the elephant home ... what the?!!!" a stone had just flew past his ear.

Stew was stood with catapult in his left hand thrust out in front of him ... the elastic from his mother's knickers dangled and bounced, attached to the weapon.

"What are you doing?" I screamed.

"Getting us some time, come on. We'll cross the island and escape off that side." he started scrambling up the small rise.

"What about Panzer?"

"Pansy? Ditch her!" he called as he used his catapult again to devastating effect, there was a scream from some security personnel in the dark.

"Bye Panzer..Pansy..Mindy..oh..gotta go, bye bye." I patted the wonderful creature on her trunk and turned. I made one step when the same trunk wrapped itself around my waist.

"No..no..no..gotta go, Mindy..let go."

I was pulled up towards her face, in the darkness I could see her small, dark, inquisitive eye. It roamed in the socket as she stared at me, taking in who I was ... then just as quickly as I was grabbed, I was released. I was placed back on the ground gently. I stared back then turned and ran, my bits swinging gently beneath me in the cool breeze of the morning, it was quite refreshing if truth be told ... note to self, kilt to be added to Christmas list later this year!

Stew continued to launch stones from his homemade catapult as we made our way across the island. He handed me his kukri, I had taken it reluctantly ... and only on the understanding I was only going to use it to get through the dense thickets.

We could hear more vehicles arriving as we struggled through the underbrush, we were scratched and hindered, but suddenly the water of the lake appeared and we knew we were not far from an escape.

"We are just gonna have to get in and get across as quick as possible, there's a hole in the fence just to the left." Stew gasped out as we got clear.

"I'm going to swim, it'll be faster." I sat down on the muddy bank and slipped into the freezing water. "Oh..my..God it's cold. I doubt if I will be able to have children when I get older."

"I'd forget about kids, it's just as unlikely you will ever kiss a bird ... never mind get one up the duff!"

119

Stew slid in and we began a slow but steady breaststroke to freedom. The noise from the police got louder, someone had obviously turned up with a loud hailer. They called for us to be sensible, (I must look that word up in the dictionary when I get home), they told us that people from the circus were here and they were crossing in a boat. This just made us happy, they were not checking the back door we were about to leave through, without saying goodbye.

"Oh no...!" Stew spluttered.

"What?"

"I've dropped my Magnum!" his handgun was sinking through the water, it had fell from his waistband.

"We haven't got time to look for it Stew, come on." I stood and walked the last few yards to the bank and pulled myself free, water cascading from my clothes and hair creating a large puddle at my feet. Stew landed a few seconds later, his face had disappointment written all over it.

"I'm coming back tomorrow with a fishing rod." He declared as he scratched an arrow into the stonework that surrounded the whole lake. "I'll know whereabouts it is now."

"Come on, let's skedaddle, before they spot us." I headed for the green metal fence that separated the lake from the park.

We felt along until we found one of the metal bars missing and this allowed us to bend and squeeze through and get away from the authorities.

Beyond the fence was heavy trees for a few yards then a steep fall down into the hollows, we jogged down, slowing ourselves occasionally by grabbing branches on bushes or pushing of the trunks of various varieties of trees. My feet went from under me on a damp patch of mud and I landed on my backside and what was left of my shorts rode up around my waist as I slid downwards like a bobsleigh champion on the Cresta run ... although I had no sled and the ground tore shreds out of my bare backside.

"Stop squealing!" Stew shouted after me.

I did stop, but only when my legs were separated by a tree stump! Tears rolled down my cheeks as I gasped for air ... I turned onto my stomach and felt my backside, it was grazed ... deeply ... it felt like a relief map of Snowdonia, peaks and troughs of pain had been chiselled out of both cheeks.

"I think I've ripped my bottom open, I have way more holes in it than when I woke up this morning." I declared to who stood over me with no pity on his face. He had slalomed down the hillside like Franz Klammer ... it was sickening.

"Are you alright?"

"I can walk, but I can't feel my bottom."

"That's okay then, don't need to feel your bottom to walk. Come on, let's get home."

I stood, pulled down my shorts as far as I could. They had now taken on the appearance of a grey miniskirt, my jumper had been lost somewhere in the scramble for freedom, and with no light, I could only imagine what I looked like ... my mind did not paint a pretty picture.

We followed the small stream at that ran between the two steep sides of the valley we were in. Stew suspected it would bring us out somewhere near the bridge, but explained that there might be police at the exit.

"What will we do?"

"We'll just go under the bridge and up the hill to Carters field and out onto Moston Lane that way."

"We'd better hurry, I think it's getting lighter ... at this moment, darkness is our friend."

"Ha ha, darkness is our friend ... where did you read that?"

"Err, in one of my dad's 'Commando' war comics, read it on the bog the other day."

"Oooh, I love them, what was it about?"

"Special services in Norway, they blew up a train with Nazi's on it!" I explained as we walked on.

"Poor Nazi's!" he said sadly.

"Stew, why do you like Nazi's so much? They were the baddies!"

"They had smashing uniform's though, and their National anthems better than ours ... and have you heard Hitler's speeches?" he explained.

"I don't speak German...!"

"You don't have too ... 'Miner dumpfer sine dinker verspallen ... der ist ine poumpernickle!" he threw his head to and fro and as he shouted out as he thumped his fist on an imaginary plinth.

"What was all that about?"

"Nothing, I made it up. But bet you had a sudden urge to invade Poland after listening to it, didn't you?"

"Yeah, had to stop myself from running straight round to Mrs. Sheminsky's house and loot her coal shed!"

"I know. But Hitler's even better than me, though! I've got a 12 inch L.P. of his best speeches ... come round tomorrow and have a listen."

"I don't know, Stew? I don't think my dad would be happy."

"He wasn't all bad ... he built the Autobahn ... the Beetle car and err..." as he thought of Adolf's plus points I interjected.

"Belsen..!!!" the silence was deafening. We walked on without speaking until a clearing appeared ahead, the darkness was now down to just a gloom ... there was a soft white mist that hovered over the grass. Ahead we were able to pick out the path.

"Let's check if there's anyone guarding the bridge." I said.

I wandered along the edge of the tree line and looked for any policemen. It appeared to be clear.

"Come on, there's no one about." I called back to Stew.

We walked slowly off the grass onto the tarmacked surface of the path and ran up to the bridge. We stopped and stared as far as we could see up the hill to the exit, it was human free. A grey squirrel darted out into the middle of the path, looked around at us and froze. Once we took a step in its direction it sprinted to a tree and jumped three feet up and disappeared to the other side of the trunk.

"We better jog up, it's time we got home, Hammy." Stew said.

"I know, but my bits are swinging all around under my shorts!"

"You worried about the squirrel spotting your nuts?" he laughed and began running.

I tutted and followed, my run was hindered by both buttock injuries and the awkward feel to being uncovered downstairs.

We reached Worsley road and took a sharp right, made our way up through ginnels to Moston Lane. Crossed over to Moston College and made our way to the sports fields to the rear. We walked across the football pitches that backed onto the college and came out near Lily lane school.

When I climbed the fence Stew was in tears … not pain or emotion. No, it was at the sight, in the new light of the morning, of my 'clawed arse,' as he put it. My juvenile meat and two veg were millimeters from being ripped off by the pointy bits that lay atop the meshed fence I got stuck atop. While he bounded over like a chimpanzee, I climbed like a grandmother! A paraplegic grandmother, with seven fingers missing!

We walked across the Diggy and eventually came upon Lakin Street, the street where we both lived. I bade him a tired farewell slipped through the back gate, then crept in the back door. No one was up! I tiptoed back up to my room and removed my clothes and stared in disbelief at the shredded shorts. Having no indoor bathroom facilities it meant I had to go back downstairs to the kitchen to wash the mud from my legs and body. I binned the shorts and put some TCP on my wounded buttocks ... the pain was shocking ... and T.C.P. can sting if it finds a way to your todger! Finally I got back to my room and lay down, sleep was only seconds away.

"Brian ... Brian, come on wake up." I had only been asleep around about four minutes it seemed.

"Dad, can I have a lie in, I'm really knackered." I begged.

"No, come on, its 11 O'clock ... here, a nice bacon butty ... and a surprise."

"Oooh..." I sat up, bacon butty and a surprise, my backside stung like I had locked 10,000 wasps in my pajamas bottoms before sleep. "...what is it?"

"I've only got tickets for the circus....!!!" he held up three tickets just in front of my disbelieving eyes.

We sat on the front row, dad, Stew and me. We glanced at each other as each act appeared, dad was having a ball and laughing like a drain at the clowns. Woooing in amazement at the bravery of the trapeze acts, the girls were well fit too, Stew said. But no elephant act yet ... but near the end, the man in red with the big top hat announced that the escape artist appearing tonight would not be a man or woman, but young Mindy who had been missing for 48 hours. Everybody stood up and cheered, we felt obliged to do the same, taking care not to drop our candy floss, pink and fluffy.

"Flipping heck, she's coming out." I whispered to Stew.

"I know, how weird is this?"

"Very..."

"Ladies and Gentleman, here tonight for your delectation, our young misfit ... Mindy the Acrobatic Elephant!" he turned and stared to his right, then flung out his right arm theatrically. The beams of light, not dissimilar to the torchlight that found us just last night, found a bounding beast coming into the ring. By her side was a man in a tight gold uniform, he skipped and shouted until they took centre stage. Mindy was suited in a similar get up to the man by her side, she had a gold helmet with a large feathered plume coming out of the centre.

The ringmaster danced off and Mindy began performing her headstands, balancing on platforms and standing on her two back legs like a begging dog. The crowd went wild, cheering each trick, then the man jumped onto her neck and began circling the ring next to the crowd, taking the plaudits, bowing arms wide as he shouted out in some Slavic tongue to Mindy.

"We could have done better than that, Bri!" Stew said.

"Well, I don't know, you couldn't even get her to lift her leg!" I stated.

"No ... but I got her to Freedom Island ... that's got to be better than standing on a flipping box!"

I turned and stared at my small friend, he didn't look back at me, he just followed the elephant as she got closer. His arms folded across his chest, candy floss stuck out at an angle, unhappy that someone had taken his toy of him. I could feel the actual seat vibrating under my sore backside as Mindy picked up speed, she was close now, I dipped my head so I didn't catch her eye. It was then I heard Stew.

"Panzer...!" and a whistle, I looked up to see the elephant coming to a halt, the guy on her back flying through the air like the trapeze artists...and landing like the human cannonball. The elephant turned and looked along the front row and moved in ... the trunk found Stew first, then me ... big sniffs ... ruffling of hair and the loss of candy floss ... and then the loudest cheer of the night.

"Told you ... that trick was better than standing on a box!" Stew laughed as Panzer snuggled his big head between the pair of us ... one eye each.

A POLISH WIND

"I do appreciate this Mrs. Skeminsky."

"Iz okay, he good boy." the fat Polish lady patted me heavily on the head. My mother bent down to talk to me.

"Listen, you behave or you're for the high jump." she pulled a handkerchief from her sleeve and put it in her mouth, then began scrubbing around my mouth. "... Jam, how is that even possible? I didn't even give you jam for breakfast!"

"Mum, mum, gerroff!" her hand held my head firmly as she rubbed harder. "I don't want your 'goz' on my face!"

"I swear I need sandpaper to get this face clean ... scruffy beggar that you are. I'm so ashamed."

"Iz okay, iz boy. Should be dirty." the large lady had a sheen of sweat on her cheeks and brow, she took my other hand, keen to get off the doorstep.

"I'll be back at about one o'clock, is that alright?"

"Iz okay, iz okay if later." she shrugged as my mum let my hand go and smiled at me, was that guilt I spied in her eyes? She was a working mum and school was closed for the day.

"Okay, be good, do as Mrs. Skeminsky says, okay?"

"Yeah, go, mum, I'll probably just play out."

Mum turned with regret and headed towards Lightbowne Road and Charlie's, the corner convenience store, where she worked.

"Breen, come in." I followed, her hand pulled firmly. Her fingers had the texture of five Cumberland sausages left out in the spring heat, moist and ever so slightly sticky.

"I'll play out Mrs. Nijinsky, if you don't mind."

"Nijinsky, iz horse, cheeky boy!" she let my hand go and carried on into the house. There was a heavy smell of Polish sausage … and cabbage.

"So, is it okay if I go out?" I turned slightly towards the door, pointing weakly.

"You go out after porzadki, okay?" she wandered towards the kitchen.

"Por... erm …" must be some breakfast, lovely. I sat at the dark oak table, it had a white lace table cloth and large candelabra with unused candles in five of the six positions available.

"Breen, what you do?" her fat, confused face appeared at the kitchen door. I sat, knife and fork in hand looking hungry.

"I'm, erm, waiting for the Porkzinky." I smiled in anticipation.

"Nie," she shook her head and her jowls wobbled, "here." she urged me to join her.

I took a small look to my left, then my right, as if looking for someone to explain. As I was alone I thought it best I bowed to her wishes. I slipped from the chair and wandered towards the kitchen. I passed a lot of dark photographs of people from what appeared to be the 17th Century in peasant clothes holding root vegetables like they were new born babies. A large picture of the present Pope beside a wooden crucifix on the wall.

"Coming, Mrs. Smimski."

I walked into the kitchen, she stood like a magician, and I was half expecting a 'tadaaaa!' Her arms were wide as she framed the mound of potatoes on the table, they sat in a bowl of water. To say I was confused would not express fully how I felt … was I supposed to eat raw spuds? Move them for her?

"Skorki…" she announced proudly. I smiled.

"Skorki..." I repeated what I thought was the word for potato with a big grin, she was teaching me Polish. "Po..ta...to…" I reciprocated, she wanted to learn the English words.

"Skorki…" this time she said it with a peeling utensil in her hand. My blood ran cold.

"Skorki?" I stared at the peeler as it came towards me in her pork sausage fingers.

"Tak! Yes, iz skorki.." she handed me the peeler, it was six inches long and appeared to have been handed down from the early iron age.

She wanted me to peel the flaming potatoes. I stared from potatoes to peeler several times as she placed a large pan of water next to me.

"En here, skorki, then en here." she pointed from potato to pan. I nodded weakly, had my mother sold me into slavery? The last thing I expected on a day off from school was to be blinking skorking!

130

Mrs. Skeminsky started singing gaily in her Slavic language, a big smile spreading across her basketball sized face.

"Hej, tam gdzies z nad czarnej wody...la la la ..."

Her voice belied her body size, close your eyes and you were in the presence of an East European angel, open them and it was a Shot Putter, closed Angel ... open ... shot putter, closed angel.

"What you do with eye?" she said, you having stroke?" she asked.

"No, no, I'm okay. I'm just a little confused Mrs. Sikorsky, am I actually 'sposed to peel all these spuds?"

"Yis, peel." she motioned an imaginary peeler across an invisible potato, the indicated to the pan. "Iz good."

"Good?" she was surely using the English language completely incorrectly. How in high heaven is peeling some potatoes good?

"Yis, good. You like me sing?"

"Erm, do you know any Sandy Shaw?"

"Shandy Saw, nie." she pushed out her bottom lip in thought. "Bibby Vinton?" she asked.

"Bibby?" I inquired.

"Nie, Bibby ... BIBBY Vinton?" she just said 'Bibby' louder "Ze Polska Prince."

"Bibby Vimto?" again I looked around for someone to translate.

"Not Bibby, Bibby! Singer, Polska singer, he in hit parade with Roses are Red, song." she began her rendition. I shrugged my little shoulders and nodded.

131

"Kielbasa?" she asked.

"Sing what you want missus, but can I play out after these spuds are done?"

"No."

"NO!!?" I exclaimed.

She shoved a large sausage towards me, if it had of been shorter it would have been camouflaged perfectly by her chubby digits.

"Kielbasa, sozeege, yez?"

"Oooh, sausage, lovely. The heavy and pungent sausage was handed to me. Then a small sharp knife.

"Ciecie!" she made a cutting motion then lifted her hand to her mouth, her lips spread wide as she pretended to chew.

I obliged, cutting a slice of the dense meat from the ring of sausage and planting it in my mouth. There was so much flavour released than from a simple pork sausage. My eyes opened wide in delight as the unctuous oils and garlic and herbs melted and spread across my moist tongue.

"Iz good?" she smiled.

"Iz flipping great!" I agreed.

"Now, 'pale'!" she nodded at the pile of spuds indicating it was time to peel.

"Okay," I agreed reluctantly.

The next hour was a surreal period of time. A Polish woman in a large pinny, with grey hair and odd slippers, (they appeared to have been peeled from the back of a live camel), sang a selection of Polish folk songs whilst I peeled potatoes and carrots, and after each vegetable I would slice off a nice piece of sausage.

132

Her cabbage rolls that were offered up as a mid-morning snack were not as good on the eye as they were on the lips and a soft drink of rhubarb and honey that I initially thought was Tizer was surprisingly refreshing.

"Come boy." I rose from my seat, stomach full and my appetite sated.

"Okay, Mrs. S." I walked to the back door with her. She lifted the latch and pulled the flimsy door hard because it had swollen slightly and stuck in the frame. "Now, you bring 'cool'."

I pushed my shoulders back and burped.

"Excuse me!" I apologised for my bad manners.

"Zokay, burp is good, mean you like."

"Cool?" I asked as I tried to see round her barrel like body.

"Yis, bring in my cool, for feer." my heart sank. Although she fed me well, each course had a price to pay. "Dog not bite!" she explained about the yellow, patchy haired, hound who was just starting to reveal large fangs as his lips peeled back … a deep throated growl made my buttocks clench up.

"Are you sure?"

"Not bite! On chain!" she pointed at the chain attached to a very rusty and infirm looking washing line post.

"What if he gets off chain?"

"He bite!" she said simply.

"He bite?"

"Yis, he bite, but chain!" she pointed confidently at the chain again.

"You better be right missus." I said as she handed me a coal scuttle.

I carefully dropped to the yard floor and took a cautionary step towards her coal shelter. The dog went berserk, I mean proper mental. He almost strangled himself as he pulled on the chain, gargling and gasping in pain such was his desire to tear me limb from limb.

"If he free, I throw sausage!" the Polish lady said as if this would ease my mind. When I looked, the sausage was in her hand whilst she took a large bite out of it. "Be okay," she chewed. "Chain strong."

"What about the post?"

"Ha, not zo strong!" Slavic shoulder shrug.

I reached the coal shelter and began filling the metal bucket blind, I was too busy watching the hound from hell screech and snarl at me while thick gobs of saliva dribbled down its hairy cheeks. I say hairy, on closer inspection I noticed it had a terrible case of alopecia, bald patches all over its body.

"Cichy, CICHY..." she screamed at the dog. I felt like I was having a preview of Hell, and here I was collecting the coals for the furnaces. The dog squealed as a knuckle from a half eaten ham hock hit it square on top of his head. It stopped spun wildly and searched out the foods resting place and instantly began crunching away on the thick, dense bone. God, the teeth on this creature were awesome, the jaw power was equal to that of a velociraptor, splinters of bone flew in all directions as he gnawed it to obliteration.

I quickly filled the bucket while I was distracted and heaved it across the yard.

"Is this enough?" I asked.

"Iz okay." she said through her sausage filled mouth.

"Can I play out now, please?"

"Yis, not go away far. Okay?"

"No, I'll stay in the street, promise." I washed myself clean of coal dust and breathed a heavy sigh of relief as I escaped out of her front door.

I burped again, cabbage filling my nostrils.

"Bugger, that came from a long way down." I declared, thinking Mrs. S would be happy with that one.

My stomach rumbled and I had the feeling of an internal landslide in my lower intestines. Then another rumble, a little louder this time.

"Buggering 'eck!" I grabbed my stomach. It was hard, like an over inflated football, the old type with leather panels, it felt like the stitching was strained to snapping point. I loosened my shorts by unbuttoning them. "Flaming Nora," I kept blowing out now trying to release some pressure.

Mrs. Neary from the last house on Douglas Street was walking up from her house, shopping bag in the crook of her arm. She looked at me, I was bent like a pen knife and groaning.

"Are you alright, Brian?" she asked.

"Orrrrgh, it's me guts, Mrs. Neary."

"What's wrong with them?"

"I feel like someone's stuck a foot pump up me bum ... and won't stop pumping it!"

"Do you have to be so descriptive....?" then she hopped back. She was a very, very large woman and

135

hopping back was not something she did lightly, literally. But she must have moved backwards four feet in a split second as my backside exploded. There was a ripping noise as the wind escaped … it was the fart from a large bull elephant, one fed on beans and cabbage for a month and one that had a large cork rammed in its backside so the gases could not escape.

"Oh my God!" I said in relief.

"Oh my good God!" Mrs. Neary said in fear.

Then the smell arrived, how it got to our noses was beyond me … it was surely too heavy to rise. If it had had a colour to it I imagine it to have been not dissimilar to mustard gas. It should have fell to earth and spread like treacle.

"Oh Lord! Is that smell you?"

"Ulp," I did a dry heave. "Yeah, sorry, I erm...phew...God I needed that."

"You dirty, dirty boy! Disgusting … you need a good raking out, it smells like a rat has crawled up your backside and died." she crossed the street and carried on to the shops muttering about what my mother must be feeding me.

Sitting on the low wall outside Number 3 Douglas Street, I let my bottom hang over the back of the brickwork as over the next hour or so I gently deflated myself, slowly and carefully in fear of any follow through. The sweating had subsided as did the fear of requiring any stitches from the initial explosive build up of wind. I couldn't, though, stop blowing making my lips vibrate. I don't know if that was just relief at not becoming airborne or an attempt at second escape route for my internal gasses.

"Breeen, Breeen…" my heart nearly stopped as I looked across at the big Polish woman's house. There she stood, large and with the look of a farmhand. Waving a large sausage ring in her right fist.

"Lunch time, Breen! I have more of my lovely cabbage rolls too, hurry boy, hurry … Breen! Where you go? Boy! Boy! Why he run?" she took a large bite at the dark red sausage without looking at it and shook her head until it broke from the body of the meat. "Dziwne Angielski! So strange these English." she then looked carefully at the sausage again as if she was looking for a landing spot, then lifted her left leg ever so slightly as she farted, not as violently as mine, but certainly as rancid. She smiled as if she had just sunk a long pink ball on Pot Black then bit another chunk off the sausage. She turned and returned inside, through her munching came that angelic singing voice … and then another fart!

Kidnapped

The morning was bright, but not quite as bright as what Stew believed he was. Nothing was that bright, his brain glowed in his skull like a 10,000 watt bulb.

Of course this meant there was almost certainly trouble on the horizon for him, me and anyone that came into any peripheral contact with him or his ludicrous plan.

"It's a no-brainer!" Stew said, this would almost certainly be the most truthful statement of the day.

"I don't know, Stew. Kath ain't gonna be happy."

"We are doing her a favour, Dave needs a walk in his pram."

These were the days when David Marsden was very young, an 18 month old, blonde haired cherub at maximum. Kath, his mother, had parked his pram outside the house with him sound asleep in the Silver Cross after a good feed.

"Should we not have told her? Or more realistically asked her?" I suggested as I walked by Stews side.

"Kath has this blinkered view of me, Hammy. She seems to think I am a bad influence on all the Marsy's, on all humanity, if I'm honest. This will make her see me in a whole new light."

"As a kidnapper?"

"Oh you of little faith!" he said with genuine sadness in his voice.

"Stew, my faith in you was obliterated a long, long time ago."

"And yet here we are on our way to the Church fayre, together!" he beamed a lipless smile at me.

"Faith has gone but you are still my mate." I tried to reason … whether that was to him or me, I'm not sure to be honest.

"And you'll get a share of the spoils if we win anything."

"50/50?" I asked hopefully.

"Ooooh, no, no, no, it's my plan!" he said quickly without even turning to face me. "70/30!"

"70/30?!" I spluttered incredulously.

"Yep, cos it'll be 90/10 if the sugar hits the fan … and 90% of that sugar we land on me, you watch."

"Okay." there was no arguing with that deal. Punishment was always unfairly dealt out when we fell afoul of our parents, so it was only fair that he took the lion's share of any rewards especially as the results rarely fell in our favour … if ever.

We left Douglas Street pushing the snoozing blonde haired child, and turned left onto Lightbowne Road. We stopped at the small advertising board that showed the latest movies showing at the Fourways cinema. On it was a child sticking two fingers up at the camera, he looked a little like us, borderline ragamuffin and definitely not heading to any Grammar school. Kes was to start showing next week and we knew it would be hard getting in to see it as we had heard it had bad language and naked buttocks in the film.

"He gets an eagle and teaches it to kill people." Stew wrongly explained the plot to me.

"He gets an eagle? From Tib Street?"

"No, he, err, he climbs a mountain and nicks a baby from the nest and then that baby eagle thinks he's his dad. Then he goes round getting all the grown-ups at school that have made his life hell."

"Sounds like an X-rated film, why is only an AA?"

"Erm, because the grown-ups don't die! They only have their eyes ripped out!"

"I don't know if I want to see that?" I squirmed.

"Pffft, what are you like? Check your pants, Hammy, make sure you have got lads bits! You even cried when Bambi's mum died!"

"That was really sad!"

"Lassie Come Home?" he continued.

"That's sad too, especially when he actually comes home!"

"Greyfriars Bobby?"

"Is that the one where the dog lies on his master's grave?" I asked with my scrunched up in thought.

"Yep!"

"Saddest of them all!" I actually felt a lump in my throat at the devotion and love that dog retained to his lost owner after the old man had popped his clogs. Oh to be loved that much.

"Come on, you push the pram." he pushed the blue pram forward on the path and let me run to stop it going onto Lightbowne Road.

"Why do I have to push him?" I called back to him when I was in control of the perambulator.

"You're 75% bird, you'll enjoy it! Plus if you are getting a 25% share, you can earn it!"

"I am not a bird."

"You are, I'm like that Kes kid, and you are my eagle!"

"You don't half talk some carp!" I pushed the handle of the pram down so I could get a good look inside. Dave was well away with the fairies, lost in the Land of Nodd.

"Come on, Pretty Polly, it starts in twenty minutes." Stew sang as he skipped passed me laughing.

Standing on the corner of Kenyon Lane, we nudged each other in genuine excitement. On the other side of the road was Saint Luke's Church grounds. A large red brick wall hid most of the fete, but over the top of the wall we could see the tops of the stalls with bunting and flags fluttering occasionally in the sporadic breaths of wind.

Crossing Kenyon Lane carefully so as not to add the charge of 'baby slaughter' to our kidnapping crime we headed to the gate where a small dissipating queue slowly passed out of view into the grounds.

"Come on." Stew grabbed the pram from me and pushed it through the gate opening.

"Hello, what have we here?" a large woman in a floral dress asked as she pushed her head into the pram to investigate.

"He's asleep!" Stew said sharply. The woman withdrew and looked at him.

"Oh, it's you!" she looked suspiciously at Stew then back into the pram at Dave.

"It's me brother!" Stewart explained.

"Oh! He's got blonde hair!" she said looking at Stews swarthy, dark skin tone and hair.

"He was born in Sweden!" he explained.

"I see!" at first it seemed a reasonable explanation but then she looked genuinely confused. Stew pushed David leaving her looking at his disappearing frame heading into the Church grounds. She turned slowly and looked at me.

"I was only born in Ancoats, Miss."

"Very good…" she had had enough and waved me through. "No messing about in there." she shouted as an afterthought.

"No, Miss, scouts honour." I promised.

I jogged up to Stew who had located the big stall he was interested in. I looked up at the legend that ran across the banner over the stall … BEAUTIFUL BABY COMPETITION! My cheeks inflated as I blew out all the air from my lungs. Stew was leaning over a desk. A tiny, middle aged woman sat looking up at Stewart, she glanced down at a clipboard in her hand.

"I do not have a child by that name on my list!" she said in a sing songy Irish lilt.

"Well, miss, my mother put my brother into the competition and now she's ill with Dengue Fever and she may even die! She really wants my brother to be in the competition."

"Dengue Fever? Has she been to Africa?" she said adjusting her glasses as if that would help her see this situation a little clearer.

"Yes, she was writing a book on Tarzan ... she needed to go an' see where he lived, then she got bit. Now she's got the Dengue Fever."

"Oh deary me, what bit her?" the woman asked with a concerned tone in her gentle Irish voice.

"What bit her?" he looked lost for a second.

"What sort of creature is it that gives you the Dengue Fever?" she reiterated.

"It was a fly, you know that horrible one!"

"A fly, a horrible fly?"

"That's it, the 'testi' fly! It bit her and gave her the Dengue fever.

"Oooh, that's awful. I never realised how dangerous a fly could be. The 'testi' fly? I don't think I've ever heard of that one. You poor little boy, please give your mother my best and tell her I will light a candle for her this evening."

"I will tell her, miss, but we don't need any candles, we have got 'lectric lights in our house."

"Oh, no ... in the church." she patted Stews grimy hand as she spoke, smiling at the miscomprehension written all over his face.

"Is that 'cos you don't have 'lectric lights in the church?" Stew asked, still having difficulty

143

understanding what the connection between his mum and a lit candle was.

"We do," she took a patient breath. "I'll be lighting a candle and saying a prayer so God can send her some love and care while she is ill." she smiled.

"Are candle's good for that sort of thing?"

"They are, now, let's get your brother registered before its too late ... name?" she picked up a pen.

"Stewart."

"Now ... is that your name or your brother's name!" she smiled again, but her Celtic patience was thinning by the second.

"Oh, you want my brother's name, don't you? His name is Ivanhoe!" he beamed with pride at David's new moniker.

"Ivanhoe ... well, I'll be, now he's the first Ivanhoe I've ever met." she said looking slightly mystified why anyone in Moston would name their child after a knight from a Sir Walter Scott novel written in the 19th Century.

"Yes, my mum wrote a book about him too!" he said proudly.

"Who, Ivanhoe?"

"Yep. She's a great writer my mum!"

"But he's not real!"

"Who ain't real?"

"Ivanhoe... "

"Who 'sez' he's not real? He's been on telly ... The Saint played him!"

"Yes, but he's just a character out of a book, isn't he? A very famous one, but he's just a romantic knight in a book by Scott." she said calmly.

"Scott of the 'Hantharhic'?" Stew asked, the lady shook her head.

"No, Sir Walter Scott!"

"Yeah ... erm, there is that book by Captain Scott. A lot of people thought that he wasn't a real person until my mum did her research and found out he was real and wrote her book that showed that he was just as real as Robin Hood and King Arthur, so there." he replied defensively.

"I ... erm ..." she looked at the poor boy, almost certainly in a state of trauma brought on by his mother being hospitalised and on death's doorstep. She decided not to cause him any more emotional turmoil. "...well, I am glad you told me, Stewart, you have taught me something today and I thank you." she said gracefully.

"Oh, erm, that's alright. I like to teach people things. I think if you can help 'heducate' someone, you should."

"Thank you!" she said, slightly offended being compartmentalised into the uneducated bracket.

"S'fine', I know other things about the Second World War and Genghis Khan if you are interested?" He offered.

"No, I think we should get little Ivanhoe registered so he can take part in the competition."

"Yeah, good idea." he looked up to see a posse of young woman arriving with their 'bonny' babies, all ready for the competitions start.

145

"So, what's his surname?"

"Sir name? He's not been knighted! He's not called Sir Ivanhoe! That would be stupid! Although..." he mused before looking at her carefully to check for any signs of sarcasm.

"I know he's not a Knight of the Realm. I mean his what is his second name."

"Oh, right, his second name is..." he stopped and looked up to the sky for inspiration.

"His surname is Donohoe...!" I butted in over his shoulder. The woman started to write then looked up at my smiling face that lay on his left shoulder next to Stewart's not so happy fizzog.

"Ivanhoe Donohoe!??" she said slowly as she wrote, she emphasised both 'hoes'.

"Yep, I'm Stewart Donohoe and this is my brother Ivanhoe." Stew explained pointing at Dave.

"How unique."

"Thank you." I said and patted Stew on his head.

"Are you family too?" she asked me.

"Yes, this is my brother, Fokker!" Stew said before I could answer in the negative,

"I beg your pardon?"

"You see our mum, the famous writer, she's German, her dad designed fighter planes in the Second World War, that's why I know so much about it."

"Fokker?" I whispered in disbelief into his ear. He ignored me but I could tell he had a Cheshire cat grin ready to split his head in half.

"Well I never!" she gasped. "Ivanhoe, Fokker and ... Stewart!"

"You never what, miss?" Stew asked.

"Doesn't matter, I hope it's you that is holding the baby and not your big brother Fo…" she stopped, she could not bring herself to say it.

"My big brother? No, our Fokker's a year younger than me!" she looked at us and I could see the struggle in her eyes, I was at least 4 inches taller than Stew and fifty per cent heavier. "No," Stew answered "I'll be holding our Ivanhoe, miss."

"Jolly good. Here, pin this on your brothers top." she handed a small piece of paper with the number 13 printed on it to Stew. He turned and started to attempt to put it on my mustard coloured t-shirt.

"On the baby, not on your big brother."

"Ahhh, yeah, wouldn't make sense pinning it on our Fokker, would it?"

"Do you really have to keep saying his name?" she was wincing each time he said it.

"What else can I call him? That's his name!"

"You can call me by my middle name! Try calling me Bri like everybody else does!" I suggested strongly.

"But I think Fokker suits you!" he was relishing the elderly woman's over the top twitch's each time he said it, and each time he said it got just a little louder than before.

"Take your baby and go and sit on the chair that has the number 13 laid on it, please." she shooed us both away.

"Fokker?" I hissed at him as we walked away.

147

"Ivanhoe Donohoe?" his hiss was just as accusatory as mine. "Now that just sounds potty!"

"Well ... you can't just stand there and not know your surname ... you would have looked mad!"

"Why not just say Smith?"

"Donohoe is the first name that popped in my head."

"It rhymes though! It like saying my name is Stewart Pewart or your name is Brian Ryan ... nobody rhymes their kids names."

"Nobody calls their kid Ivanhoe either!"

"I will!" he declared.

"Nobody normal calls them Ivanhoe!"

Stewart leaned into the pram and began prising David from under his blanket.

"Come on, Da... erm, Ivanhoe." he lifted him up and to his chest. David, who's hair was now statically stood up like Albert Einstein's after reacting to Stewarts non-natural fibre jumper, clung tightly as tightly as possible to Stewart with his tiny fingers wrapped into the 'v' of his grey top. He looked around nonplussed. He sucked hard on the dummy that was in his mouth several times and then focused on Stewart face as if he had just noticed he wasn't his mother.

"Hello, Dave." Stew said softly. "Are you gonna win us the big prize with your lovely smile?" Dave decided it was time to start to cry!

"Oh flipping 'eck!" I said backing off slightly.

"Don't cry Dave. Dave, Dave what's wrong?" Stew bounced him lightly in his arms. "Hammy, go and find a rusk, or a banana or a sausage ... and be quick!"

While Stewart took his seat on the stage with the now sobbing child I raced off into the ever building crowd on a mission.

As luck would have it Denise Connell, a tiny, flame haired girl of 11 who lived on the corner Douglas Street came into view ... pushing her baby brother, Gerrard, in a small pram. He was wrapped up in a warm baby grow and on his head was a green knitted bobble hat, five sizes too big. She smiled in recognition and I returned a beaming smile.

"Hello, Hammy."

"Hi, Denise. What you doing?"

"I'm walking round St Luke's fete!"

"Yeah, sorry, course you are. Is this your new brother?"

"Yeah, it's our Gerard. Little crying git!"

"He's not crying!"

"He's all right as long as he's got that bottle in his mouth."

"What's in the bottle? Milk?"

"Warm milk and rusk, he loves it!"

"Bet you'd rather have someone else pushing him round for ten minutes, wouldn't you?"

"What d'ya mean?"

"I don't mind pushing him for a bit, if you like?" I said a little too desperately.

"What, and let me go and hang out with me mates?" her eyes gleamed at the thought of temporary respite.

"Yep, just ten minutes like, and I'll meet you back here at the Hoopla Stall." she pushed her brothers pram in front of me and started away.

"I'll take good care of him, promise." I shouted after her.

"I don't care … just don't kill him!" she shouted back and waved her left hand over her shoulder dismissively.

"Come on, Ged, let's go and meet your mate, Dave."

I pushed the lightweight pram over the grass, making Gerard buck up and down, he struggled to get the teet of the bottle that was in his hands into his ever open mouth.

"Excuse me, excuse … thank you." I called out as I made my way to the front of a small throng of women. Although dressed mainly in monochromes every one of them wore a very colourful, silk head scarf. It covered their hair and tied under their chins. 1969 glamour! They all seemed to have their arms folded and carrying a large, full shopping bag in the crook of one of said arms and each woman appeared to have the same judgmental expression as they looked on at the young mothers sat with their bonny babies on the stage … it was like a Moston version of the Stepford Wives! On the stage, amongst the mothers was a stressed out Stew and an extremely snotty and wet faced Dave Marsden … our little Ivanhoe!

"Have you got something for him to drink or eat?" he shouted across to me.

"Look." I pointed down at Gerard's bottle that was now latched onto the baby's mouth.

"Give it here." he mouthed his free hand waggling, urging God's speed.

I leaned over the pram and pulled the bottle from Ged's small clasp and held it up with a smile. Gerard burst into a wail of sadness. I looked at Stew who pleaded with me to bring him the bottle ... then at the little child in my care. I passed the bottle back to Ged, who gurgled with joy and started to suckle the fluids again.

"Hammy! Just bring me the bottle!"

I left the contented Ged and stepped onto the stage next to Stew.

"I can't, he starts screaming if I take it off him."

"We've no chance of winning with a skriking kid have we!" he explained.

"I know, I've got a plan." I said, clicking my fingers and leaving an index finger sticking up in the air.

"What?"

"We'll swap babies."

"Swap 'em for what?" he asked.

"No, you can have Ged in the competition, with the bottle ... a happy baby and no snot to boot!"

"Actually, that might work. Fling him over."

I unstrapped the contented little baby and took him to Stew.

"Take that hat off him, it looks like he's had his head shrunk!" I removed the knitted cap and placed it on David's bigger, older head, where it actually fitted a lot better.

"Yeah, this kid looks cuter." Stew said weighing up first Ged, who was now on his knee, then Dave who was dangling from my grasp.

"It's the snot that lets Dave down, I think!"

"Yeah, too much green on his face for a prize winning performance. That green hat actually matches that sludge running down his face." he laughed, stress free again.

I held Dave at arm's length and returned him to Ged's pram and strapped him.

"Let's see if there's anything to eat under here, Dave." I dropped to my knees and looked at the items in the tray under the pram. "Oh, look, there's some tissues for your runny nose … and … ooh, look, some food! Here you go." I knelt up and wiped the poor lads face until it was clear of nasal fluids then from behind my back I produced a … carrot! "Chomp on this matey!"

Dave's brow furrowed as he considered the vegetable his little hand came out and retrieved it from my grasp and took a bite on it with his fairly new teeth. He didn't look overly impressed with the flavour, but he ploughed on. Then a voice came over the tannoy. "Ladies and gentlemen, we are about to judge the Bonny Baby competition, so if you want to gather round. This year's judges will be our own lovely Vicar, Thomas Sweetbread of St Luke's, the next judge is his wife Celery … whoops a daisy, I mean Celia, sorry Celia, I've thinking about my shopping after the show, silly me."

The vicar's wife stared intently at the woman with the microphone.

"...and the final judge is our local Policeman in Moston, P.C. Farthing. He had just popped in to check everything was okay and we have asked him to help judge these gorgeous little boys and girls, thank you for helping us out, Ted." she smiled at the Policeman who was cradling a hot beverage. This was probably the real reason he had bobbed into the fete! He loved his tea! He smiled at the woman with the microphone and nodded to the small crowd.

Stew stared at me and pulled a face of disgust. He pointed at the back of the copper and mouthed 'it's 'Tithead'! I burst out laughing. Ted was a lovely amiable policeman and his lack of pace meant that he rarely bothered giving chase to young, pacey lads out nicking apples.

"Wh ... wh ... what's so funny, boy?" the copper, who had stepped forward, asked me.

"Nothing, sir, sorry!" It was his nickname that made me laugh. His mild stutter meant that if you ever asked his name it came out as 'T.. t.. tet..Ted'. Stew had insisted it sounded like he was telling you his name was Tit head!

"Stu.. stu.. pid boy, laughing at n.. ner.. nothing." he stood back in line with the vicar and his wife, and took a long drink from his tea mug, but still managing to glare at me.

I stepped back into the crowd and blew out the air that I had held for the last thirty seconds or so.

"Okay, first mother, number 1, Mrs. Scrimger and her daughter, Annabel. Oooohhh look at them eyes, she's going to be a heartbreaker isn't she?" the woman

153

held her daughter forward for the judges to assess, the vicar and his wife cooed and tickled her chin while P.C. Ted closed one eye and appeared to be checking the child for signs of foot rot rather than assessing cuteness. They all made notes on pieces of paper as they went along. Ted scratching a well-developed sideburn occasionally as he tried to look interested.

Stew was last in line and he had managed to keep little Ged happy for the fifteen minutes that it taken for the judges to reach him.

"Next is...!" the woman looked up from the paperwork attached to her clipboard and stared around until she spotted the small Irish woman who had taken our details. Off mic she asked her was the details correct ... once it had been confirmed she stood tall again and raised the microphone to her mouth.

"Sorry, our next baby is little Ivanhoe!" the crowd who had been relatively mute throughout the proceedings burst out laughing. "What an unusual name!"

"I don't think it's unusual!" Stew said defensively.

"Well, there's not many Ivanhoe's in Moston, I think." she smiled at the crowd rather than at Stew. He took this to be her mocking him and his 'brother', Ivanhoe.

"What's your name then?" he asked slightly aggressively.

"Excuse me?" she turned to give Stewart her full attention.

"I'm just asking what your name is."

"My name? My name isn't important, son." she smiled a very fake smile.

"Her name is Nora!" a voice called from the crowd. Nora swung round in an attempt to spot the culprit.

"There …" Stew said.

"There? There what?" she asked him as she re-focused.

"Nitty Nora!" he declared.

"How dare you?"

"How dare you! You made fun of our kid's name, so I'm making fun of yours. Not nice is it? Nitty Nora!"

"I did not make fun of your brother, I just said it was not a common name."

"I never heard you say that. I heard you say our kid was unusual, and that ain't nice."

"I didn't mean … I'm sorry, shall we just get on with the show?"

"You can for me … and our Ivanhoe." Stew's face changed from thunder to summer as the judges stepped forward to check his little 'sibling' out.

"Where's your mother, little boy?"

"She's on death's 'doorknob'!" he changed his expression to a sad one as he spoke. "She's got an 'orrible disease and is in bed."

"Oh, dear. So have you brought your brother to get him out of the house?" the vicar's wife asked.

"We've brought 'im so we can win the money!" he said loudly into the microphone. This caused another uproarious peel of laughter from the crowd.

"Very good, and very honest." the vicar's wife answered.

"I am honest."

"Is that you, St.. Ster.. Stewart?" the policeman scrunched up his face and puckered his lips so half his thick moustache disappeared up his enormous nostrils as he leaned over the vicars wife's shoulder to check out the face of his major nemesis on the streets of Moston.

"Is that you, Ter.. Ter.. Tithead?" the muscles in my neck that held my head upright failed as his words hit my ears, my chin hit my chest a millisecond later.

"You haven't ger.. ger.. got a bur.. bur.. brother!"

"Who says I haven't?"

"I ju.. ju.. just did! I know your der.. der.. details inside out, young lad!"

"Do you know this boy, constable? Is he Stewart…" the woman with the clipboard checked contestant number 13. "Stewart Donohoe?"

"Ner.. ner.. no! This is Ster.. Ster.."

"Spit it out, Ter.. Ter.. Ter.. Tithead!" Stewart stood and pulled Ged tight to him.

"His name is Neale!" the copper spat out.

"I thought his name was Stewart!" the vicar asked.

"Ster.. Ster.. Stewart Ner.. Neale. He's a little ver.. ver.. villain."

"Is this right? Is this your brother?"

"Not exactly my brother. But … we only live 'bout 200 yards apart!" he seemed to see this as next of kin in Moston.

156

"You are disqualified! Please leave the stage, go on."

"It's a fix!" he shouted out to the crowd.

"Hard luck, matey." a man called back through the laughter.

"Come on, our Ivanhoe." he stepped down from the stage and headed towards me. I had shrunk three sizes and barely acknowledged him when he got to me.

"I hate that copper, fat ger.. ger...get! Here take Ged, he weighs a ton!" he passed me the baby and he rolled his shoulders to loosen the muscles.

I turned to place Ged in his pram. It wasn't there! Pram and more importantly, Dave, had gone!

"Stew!"

"What now?"

"Dave's gone!"

"His prams here." he pointed at the large blue pram Dave had arrived in.

"I stuck him in Ged's pram ... and it's gone! Someone has kidnapped Dave!"

"We'll stick Ged in the pram and put it back outside Kath's. Job done!"

"Don't you think Kath will notice that it's not here son?"

"Naw, it's a known fact ... all babies look the same!"

"What about the fact that Ged has no teeth? He's bald ... and Denise won't have a baby to take home!"

"Come on, we'll go and find another baby for Denise and then everybody's happy."

"Where are we gonna find a spare baby?"

157

"I bet this happens all the time, women taking the wrong baby from outside a shop, I wouldn't be surprised if me and you are not living with our real parents."

Stew pushed a gap through the crowd and I followed with a now tired Ged lay in David's Solver Cross pram.

"I hope we don't see Denise. She'll want to know where her little pram is."

"She can have this one, its miles better. I'll bet she will be happy we have upgraded her pram."

"Stew!"

"What?" he stopped as soon as we were clear of the crowd.

"Focus. We have lost Dave. If we give Denise the pram Kath will notice … they live on the same flipping street."

"Let me think." he scratched the crown of his head. I stood with my heart beating like a jack hammer in my chest as he thought.

"Hello, boys." I stared up into the face of Billy Marsden, Dave's dad!

"Hello Ber.. Ber.. Bill." I had caught Teds speech impediment.

"Your dads over there, Bri." he pointed to the back of large slender, yet strong back of a dark haired man buying raffle tickets out of a red plastic bucket off a stall holder.

"Oh yes."

"Have you won anything?" he continued.

"Nope, we lost something!" I whispered.

"What?"

"Nothing!"

"Hey, Bill. I think this is your pram!"

"What?"

"We found this pram ... and I, er, think it's your Dave's."

"It is!"

"Where did you find it?"

"Over there." Stew pointed vaguely towards the stage against the far wall.

"Who's this kid in it?"

"It's Ged Connell. Someone's nicked his pram and probably swapped babies too!"

"What the ... where's Dave?"

"Oh, I don't know. Just know that this is his pram!"

"Brian, go and tell your dad I'll meet him in the Lightbowne later. I better take this home and find out what's going on."

Once Stew had removed Ged from the pram, Bill pushed it towards the gate. I reached my dad who was whooping as he matched the number on his raffle ticket with the ticket sellotaped to a bottle of deep yellow Advocaat on the table behind the stall holder.

"Hello, Bri. Look what I've won."

"Brill, hey dad. Bill is just nipping home..." I turned slightly to point towards where Bill had been stood. It was then I spotted Kath at the gate ... she was holding Dave in her arms. On his head was the green bobble hat. By her side looking just as angry was Denise holding an empty pram. She had obviously grabbed the

159

pram thinking Ged was in it and headed home. That's when things started to unwind. Or as Stew would say, the sugar hit the fan.

In the middle ground was Stew, alone, left holding the baby. Nowhere to run, nowhere to hide. And that is why he always got the 90% of any winnings … he was always the one that took the flak when it went wrong. Poor Stew, always on the verge of victory, but never getting across the winning line. He looked back at me and his eyes were dead. I read his lips as he spoke too quiet to be heard.

"Buggeration!"

I looked back at my dad.

"Hey, dad. Can I have a go?"

His massive right hand landed on my thick mop of hair like a wrecking ball and he rubbed heavily.

"Course you can, do you feel lucky?"

"Right now I feel very lucky, dad. Very lucky indeed!"

THE KIDD'S ALRIGHT

The daylight had started to fade away and dusk was now dim enough to coax the streetlights to pop on. Their vague orange light slowly getting brighter as their bulbs buzzed and warmed. Meanwhile inside the Hamblett family home on Lakin Street a little boy stood, buttoning up his black duffle coat. His mother is at the kitchen table writing on the back of an envelope, coins stacked neatly next to her scribbling hand.

"Brian, I'm putting the money in the envelope, don't take it out, and just give it to Mrs. Kidd." she said while physically showing me the money going into the envelope.

"Okidoki!" I replied merrily as I tried to work out why there was no buttonhole left for my last button.

"Oh, Brian, come here. You've done your coat up all wrong. I do worry about you! When will you start grasping the basic things in life like laces, buttons or zips?"

"Oh yeah." I realised my mistake and began unbuttoning until my mother took control.

"...and look!" she pointed at my trousers, zip down and white y-fronts plainly on view.

"Sorry, but it's not my fault!" I insisted.

"Is it not? Whose fault will this be? The zip fairy? Is it the buttons themselves? Is that the fault of the duffle coat company? Fancy them lining up the buttons with the button … holes? What sort of stupid system is that?" she continued as she zipped and buttoned me up. I looked on with disdain, quietly pulling my tongue out at the top of her head.

When I was wrapped up and had no privates were left on parade she pulled my hood up and covered my hair, then gently patted my head.

"Now, here's the money," she put the envelope in my pocket and patted it, "...and here is the bag, plates, and a mug, please don't spill the gravy!" she held my shoulders as she spoke and locked eyes "Do...not...swing...the bag!" she nodded waiting for a response in like.

"Okay mum, I'm not stupid." I said unconvincingly.

"Let me finish that sentence for you, Brian, I'm not stupid … all the time!" she stood up straight and felt her back, a groan left her lips.

"I know 'you're' not! he he." she gave me her withering look which I ignored. "By the way I'm not stupid … at all! I just forget things. My mind is busy a lot of the time, and no one who is interesting is ever clean or has their zips done up all the time. Them people who is organised and clean and smart … well, they have nothing going on in their lives. I'd rather think about space travel, football or arm-wrestling than whether me fly is done up or not!" I walked, swinging the bag towards the front door, my football was just showing from under the sideboard, my left foot niftily dragged it out.

162

"Hey, no football, and when the gravy is in there, remember, don't swing the bag!" mum said in exasperation.

"I'll be okay with the ball, I need to practice as much as possible if I'm going to be a top footballer ... and I can swing it now, there's no gravy in there, so stop stressing ... ouch!" I yelped as the bag suddenly connected with my right knee and the heavy, dinner plated, shopping bag carried some weight.

"Serves you right, clever clogs. Now be careful crossing Lightbowne Road, pick the ball up before you cross and use the zebra, look both ways, don't just run across ... are you listening, young man?"

"Yeah, you said blah di blah ... careful, blah di blah ... don't run ... blah di blah ... keep your eyes closed when you cross! All the obvious things that everybody does anyway!" I laughed at the glowering face that met my answer. Mum didn't do stern very well, it was like John Inman trying to be Clint Eastwood ... Dirty Harry? No! More 'make your bed', than 'make my day'!

"I think you need to show a little more respect, Brian, it's not funny saying things like, I'm going to 'keep my eyes closed' to cross the road! And what's with this blah di blah!? Is that what Stewart's teaching you? Can you stay away from that child?"

"I'm only joshing, mum. I'll be careful, I'll not talk to any people with strange puppies and I'll look both ways ... twice! With my eyes wide open when I cross the road, promise!"

"Good, now go, before there's a queue. Do you want any bread?"

"To take with me? Yes please, with jam or cheese or...what?" I was stopped by her glare.

"I mean ... do you want bread with your fish and chips when you get back!" she shook her head in despair.

"Course I do, you can't have fish and chips without bread and real butter!" I smiled as mum opened the door, squeezed past and out into the darkening evening.

I could hear the plates rattling loosely against each other in the bag as I walked and they were in really serious danger when I ran across the unchecked, main road, chasing the ball I'd forgotten to pick up. The noise became a major clattering as they threatened to beat themselves to death in my sprint for the wayward ball, but they survived as did I. One block down on the opposite side of the road, a shop window suddenly flickered with light and the door was pulled open letting steam escape out and upwards. I would be her first customer, and so a minute or so later I entered that door to Kidd's chippy. The warm light and evocative smell of fried food welcomed me in as did the proprietor, the ever lovely Mrs. Kidd.

"Hello Brian." she said and a smile broke across her face, her fringe drooping down on her forehead as the perspiration and condensation played havoc with her hair. She looked a little flustered with the manic preparation that was required for the Friday evening service. She mumbled as she looked at each department of her shop. I acknowledged her greeting as she wandered around behind the counter.

"Peas, done ... fish in ... sausages in ... pies warmed ... gravy...on..." she slowly wiped her brow with her right forearm and turned to face me. "...right Brian, I think we are all ready to go. Have you got a list off your mum?"

"Yep, the money's inside." I stood on tip toes and passed her my jangling envelope.

"Two fish and chips and a portion of mushy peas and some gravy ... pass me your bag, love." she said as she reached over to take the hessian bag. She placed the two plates on top of the fish fryer to warm and then looked over the counter at me.

"Guess who's in the back of the shop!"

"Is it Giant Haystacks?" my eyes widened in anticipation.

"Who?" she asked, slightly bemused and taken aback by my rapid answer.

"Giant Haystacks, he's a wrestler, and a giant. You must have seen him on World of Sport!"

"No, I'm always busy in here on a Saturday afternoon!" she explained.

"Oh yeah! You should get yourself a telly in here, he's brilliant, and no one beats him ... ever!"

"I'm sure he is very good, but I've no time for telly on a Saturday, it gets a little mad in here. So you're going to have to guess again, because it's not him."

"Is it ... erm ... Father Christmas? Bet he likes fish and chips!" my face lit up with hope, only five weeks until he was due down our chimney.

"No, it's not Santa. I think I'd better just tell you, it may be quicker! It's my son, he's called Brian too!" she nodded her head to her right, towards the door where she chipped her potatoes.

"What? You mean there's a footballer is in the shop? A famous one to boot, one that has scored a header in a European Cup Final!!" I pulled myself up so I could see more of the back room, but there was no sight of Brian Kidd.

"Yes, he is all that, but he also never tidied his room or put his dirty underpants in the basket … he was a right scruffy sod, to be honest!" she offered conspiratedly. "Brian, come and say hello to my favourite customer." she called into the shadows of the back room.

A man emerged, he was tall and lean and a big beaming smile he had obviously inherited off his mother, spread across his face. But the thing that sticks in my memory more than anything was his hair! Skin and bone he was probably around six feet one inch, but his hair was right out of the Hair Bear Bunch, and added a good four inches to his height.

"Hello son." his voice was warm, deep and Mancunian.

I stared in awe, words were a pick and mix in my head. They were all there, but they refused to knit together in a sentence.

"Woooah…!" I stammered.

"These are going to be a few more minutes, Brian." Mrs. Kidd said as she rustled the chips in the large range.

"Are you a United fan then, Brian?" the footballer asked.

"Err..yeah..look at your hair!" I said in amazement.

"I know, he pays nearly thirty pounds for a haircut in London and when he comes out of the barbers his hair is bigger! How does that work? More money than sense, if you ask me!" Mrs. Kidd said without turning from the fryer.

"Mum, it's not a barbers!" Kiddo explained with a beaming grin.

"I know it's not! He's a highwayman, daylight robbery. Come and sit down on this chair while I 'tease' your hair into a perm...oh, and leave your footballers wallet by the till!" she said in disgust at the waste of money.

"I think it's great!" I said to the tall footballer.

"Thank you! See mum, a man who knows where it's at!" he said to his mother's back as she shovelled crisp, suntanned chips into the holding pan.

"Oh Brian! I thought you were sensible. Where do you get your hair cut?" she asked over her shoulder.

"Steptoe's on Lightbowne Road, he's rubbish, he can only do one haircut ... and he always chops off my sideburns, it costs sixpence and its rubbish."

"Your hair looks..." she turned and looked at the dark mop sat on my head, uncombed and unkempt ... like a male Medusa ... not snakes writhing around though, more like rat tails. "...well, you're probably due a visit to him very soon. Get it cut nice and short, sensible, not all high falluting like Mr. 'Look at Me' here." she

167

laughed as she thumbed a hand at her son and returned to her chip duty.

"Give over, mum. I'm still the same as ever, I just like my hair like this … me, high falluting!? Tssk!"

"What about those shoes, you look like you are on stilts. Have you ever seen anything like them, hey Bri?" she asked me.

"I can't see, I'm too small to see over the counter." I was desperate to see the whole ensemble.

"Here…." she disappeared out of the door on her side of the counter and I heard an unbolting of the door on the customers side. "...quick in here before any other customers arrive." I followed the proprietor in the flowered tabard into the back, rolling my ball slowly, foot to foot. She bolted the door again and told me to sit at a small table. "....Brian, show him them shoes."

Kiddo walked into the back room, bending slightly so he didn't bang his head. He wore cream flared trousers that touched the floor, hiding the shoes, so he had to pull the trouser leg up to reveal what my father would call 'Claude Hoppers! A shoe with a heel of four inches and wedges under the sole of an inch or more.

"Ridiculous!" Mrs. Kidd exclaimed as she returned to her chips. "Would you like a can of pop, Brian?"

"No thanks, mum." the footballer replied.

"Not you, little Brian!" she explained.

"Oooh, yes please, Dandelion please … hey, Kiddo, I love your shoes, they're brilliant."

168

"Ha, as I said before, a man with taste." his laugh was deep, it didn't go quite right with his beanpole exterior, it was the laugh of a much heftier man.

"Thank you, Mrs. Kidd." I said as she passed me a cold can of D&B.

The back door to the chippy was open to allow some of the condensation another escape route. It opened onto a backyard, flagged, with a green painted, wooden gate.

"Come on, let's have a kick about while you wait for your chips." he held his hands out for my ball.

Like in a dream I followed this genial giant, striding like he had ten league boots on out into the dark yard.

"Why did you leave United Brian? You don't mind me calling you Brian, do you?" the ball came at me like an exocet, hard and direct. I killed the ball instantly, it dropped dead at my right foot and I rolled it back to him a couple of hundred miles an hour slower, and slightly less accurately.

"No course not, that's my name. United ... errr ... well I have and always will be a massive United fan, but it's just that my face didn't fit anymore." the ball flew towards me again and again, it was controlled easily.

"What? Was your head was too big to get through the shirt? Was that 'cos of your hair? Are Arsenal shirts bigger, then?"

"No, it's not because of my hair, good God, it's not that big!" I looked at him doubtfully as he gently stroked it.

"Have you not seen your head in the mirror? It is proper 'maffis'!" I tried to hit it back with a little more venom and took him by surprise, it hit him on the calf leaving a round, dark stain on his cream trousers.

"Sorry!"

"Its fine." he said rubbing at the mark, only making it worse. "Well I left United due to the management, I didn't want to leave, but they wanted the money from selling me more than they wanted me! Arsenal and staying in the First Division, in the end it was a no brainer and it was sorted out for me by the money men before I had time to really think."

"It's a shame 'cos we're doing brilliant now in the Second Division, top of the league and Stuart Pearson is scoring loads of goals for us. He's got normal size hair though!"

"Can we leave my hair out of this, please? I get enough grief off my mother and Bob

Wilson, without a little kid having a go at me!" he laughed. He picked the ball up and offered to throw it high. "Head?"

"Okay … no 'purly curm' talk anymore." I agreed. "Go on, high!" the ball was launched up and I headed it back into his arms. "Here, give us the ball Brian, how many can you do?" he bounced the ball to me and I immediately started flicking the ball up, from one foot to the other, not allowing any contact with the floor. I counted as I went, I reached 21 and had to overstretch and only ended up knocking the ball against Kiddo's brilliant white shirt. Another circular mark.

"Sorry, but 22, not bad, hey? Bet you can't do that in those...erm...'canal boats' you're wearing!" he looked at me after he had perused his now smudged shirt.

"Here..." he wanted the ball.

"Bet you can't even do ten in them...hehe."

Brian Kidd, professional footballer, internationally capped and winner of the European Cup only a few years earlier was about to take me on in a keepy-uppy challenge...eek!

He held the ball and then threw it out in front of him with a back-spin on it. It hit the ground and the rotation brought it back towards him with the spin, he started well, easy if not nonchalantly. Same style, left foot, right foot...each contact keeping the reverse spin going so it always stayed close in to his body. He suddenly flicked it slightly higher than he wanted, but he controlled it nicely on his knee... (another stain!)...it dropped again to his feet and he continued with his ever so simple juggle.

I counted and as each number got higher a little despair entered my voice.

"13, 14, 15, 11...!"

"Hey, that's 16 not 11, 18...19..!" he cried out, flustering him. He decided to continue the count himself.

"Brian...." his mother's call from the back door.

"Yes..." answered by both of us, followed by a slight miscontrol on the part of the biggest Bri, as he glanced up, the ball flying off at a tangent and hitting the window on the rear of the chippy.

"Hey, what have I told you about playing football in the backyard? Good God, Brian, how old are you ... 10?"

"11, Mrs. Kidd!"

"Not you, that Hefferlump there!" she checked there was no cracks in the glass.

"Sorry mum." the penitent footballer said.

"Brian...small Brian, your mums here, come on back in." she turned and hastily returned to her work.

I walked back in, arms aloft, doing a little dance of victory.

"I beat Brian Kidd in keepy uppy...ha ha ... sucker!!"

"Hey, kid, I was interrupted, watch this, come back. I can do that on my head, hey ... kid..." I could hear the ball bumping off his head. "...are you watching, 12, 13..." I ignored it and walked back through the back of the shop and unbolted the door to find my mother stood there in her pink, fluffy flip floppy, slippers.

"Where have you been? I've been worried to death!"

"Whaaat?" I've only been five minutes, you don't have to come looking for me after five minutes, I'm not a baby!"

"You've been half an hour!"

"Sorry Marie, it's my fault, I let him meet my Brian. They've been playing ... what the? Look at the state of you!" she had just spotted her colossal son in the doorway. He ignored her and leaned over the counter to me.

"Hey kid, 30 on my head and I could easily have done one hundred!" he held the ball over the counter, his hair was wet and flattened at the front onto his muddied forehead.

We all stood and stared for a second, his shirt blotched dark by the ball.

"Yeah? But did anyone see you do it?" I asked suddenly.

"What do you mean?"

"No one saw it so it doesn't count ... and I think that makes me the winner, Kiddo!"

"Brian, it's Mr. Kidd to you ... hello." mum nodded at the 'dirty' footballer.

"Look at you, Brian! Trousers ruined...shirt ruined ... hair...well that was a mess anyway!" his mother chastised him thoroughly.

"Will everybody leave my hair alone ... I like it ... okay?" he looked at each of us in turn then pulled out an afro comb to 'tease' the fringe back into a fluff ... quite unsuccessfully.

"Hey, Kiddo ... erm, Mr. Kidd, can I have your autograph?" I asked.

"Sure, but as long as you admit I did 30 on me head!" he laughed.

"Okay, you did 30." I agreed reluctantly.

Meanwhile Mrs. Kidd had wrapped our plated food in the News of the World and poured her treacle thick, gravy into the mug, all placed in the bag and handed back to mum.

Kiddo signed a large piece of white paper and passed it across to me ... it read,

173

'To Brian ... the biggest cheat in Manchester, all the best ... Brian Kidd ... Mr. 30 headers!'

"Say thank you." mum pushed me gently.

"Hey Mr. Kidd. I had my fingers crossed ... so that makes me still the winner. He he!" I declared.

"Brian ... say thank you." the push less gentle now.

"Thank you... (Loser)." I whispered with a smirk.

"I don't believe you. Have I brought you up to be rude to your elders? I'm so sorry." she apologised to the Kidd's.

"I'm not being rude, mum. Just being honest."

"It's fine, he's a good lad ... and he'll make a good footballer." he said to mum.

"Thank you. Right empty head ... let's get home before these go cold, hey?" she bade farewell to mother and son and bustled me towards the exit.

"See you Mrs. Kidd ... see you Brian. And don't forget to tell Alan Ball and Peter Marinello you got beat by a little boy. He he."

"Stop teasing him, Brian, it's not nice." I was finally hustled out of the door as I heard Mrs. Kidd laying into her son.

"Will you ever grow up? Come here, bend down." through the big front window, the one with the Holland's meat pie sign hanging proudly, I saw her licking her handkerchief and wiping mud from his head.

"Hey, look mum. I hope you don't do that to me when I grow up!"

174

"It's what mothers always do. I'll still be worrying about you when you're 50!!!" she said as we strode home, her slippers clip clopping rhythmically while carefully keeping the bag horizontal. I continued kicking the ball against the wall and controlling it as it bounced just ahead of me.

"50!! I don't think so. You'll be about a hundred, won't you?"

"Cheeky monkey, I think you can do some math's homework when you eaten your tea!" she laughed.

"I'll do it when I'm eating my tea ... I'll count me chips and make sure I've got more than you. Didn't you say you was gonna start a diet?"

"No, I did not! I said I may cut back a little ... that's not a diet!"

"Ahhh, potatoes ... tomatoes!" I misquoted the song.

"You just count your blessings...that should keep you busy until your 50. Potatoes...tomato?? Deary me, Brian, what on Earth are we going to do with you?"

"Hey, I just beat Brian Kidd at keepy-uppy, you can't knock that, mum, can't knock that ... at all!" I said proudly moments before I stepped in a large, moist dog turd. "Bugger..!"

"Oh ... Brian!"

Koo Koo Ka Choo

I had rapped on Stew's door a little too hard and the thick, pebble shaped, glass had actually hurt my knuckles. I was stood looking at them when the door finally opened.

"Hello, what have we here?" Stew's dad asked sarcastically.

"It's just me, Guy. Is Stewart coming out?" I risked a quick glance up at him as I spoke, then back to my red raw knuckles, hoping he would just turn round and go and fetch him.

"How's your dad?" he folded his arms, being careful not to spill the coffee in the brown mug he was holding.

"He's fine."

"Is he going to the pub later?" he asked now settling in for a chat, he leaned against the brickwork on the left of the door.

"He didn't say, but I would imagine he will pop out for a 'quick one'." I tried to peer round him to see if Stew was coming.

"You got a bird yet?" he smiled, and so it begins.

"No."

"You're not one of them woofters, are you?" he grinned now.

"A what...?"

"A shirt lifter ... you know ... shut that door!" he lifted his arm and patted his hand down, the universal hand sign in 1972 for a limp wrist. He lifted his eyebrows and kept them there inquisitively...appearing unsure of my reply.

"No..." I said defensively ... Larry flaming Grayson!! How dare he?

"Well, why no bird, then?" he seemed genuinely lost why I wasn't courting.

"Well ... I'm only 11!!"

"I'd had ten birds by the time I was 11 ... and I had three of them pregnant! You can't wait around forever, you know!" he looked at his nails, then brushed them on his shirt.

"I'll keep it in mind. Do you think he is he ready yet?"

"I'd go for a fat bird, for your first one ... you're a bit of a chunky monkey yourself, aren't you?" he pointed at my little pot belly.

"What do you mean?" I looked down at my zipped, brown cardigan and patted the large folded crease around my stomach.

"No. You're not fat, just carrying a bit of timber. Now that idiot..." he pointed his thumb over his shoulder down the hallway. "...like a rake, eats like a horse, never puts a pound on... costs us a fortune!"

"I know, it's not fair..." I admitted sadly to my friend's dad.

"...like I said...a nice looking tubby bird, 'cos you're not ugly, well not really ugly ... not mirror

177

breaking repugnant. You know what I mean, don't you? No offence?" he slowly crossed his arms again.

"Erm...to be honest, no, I don't know what you're on about ... I actually think I'm quite handsome!" you could hear my self-doubt in the weakness of my voice.

"Hey, that's it ... self-belief. Big yourself up ... you may grow up and look like Jason King, hey? Now he's a real lady killer. Or a rock star, like that, what's he called...erm...Gary Glistner! You know who I mean ... hairy chest and big boots!" he grinned consolingly at me as he stomped his feet to the silent leader of the 'Gang!'

"It's Glitter!" I picked the ball up from between my feet and stared at the writing on it...'Hammy is a puff!' Was there no escape from this esteem assassination?

"What is?" he looked at me confused. "What? Glitter? Is it on my face?" he wiped his chin and looked carefully at his hand for anything sparkly.

"No, the singer, it's Gary Glitter." I explained, where the heck was Stew?

"Yeah...yeah, that's the one." he pointed at me to confirm that I was right.

"Can you get Stew now, please?" I smiled pleadingly.

"Yeah, he won't be long, he's putting his new shoes on and it takes him ages to get up onto his feet!" at that precise moment the lounge door, down the hallway opened and Frankenstein's monster clumped out!

"Here he is...'Rumplestilts..on'!" he stood back and out of the gloom an image appeared.

178

"Wooooah…" I said, dropping my football, I wanted to applaud this entrance.

Stew was on the biggest platform shoes I had ever see. Three layered sole, two chocolate brown levels sandwiching a cream one … and he had an enormous star on the shoe covering the toes. His jumper was in the same colours of brown. He had three large beige stars emblazoned on the front of his dark brown jumper and at his neck was two large collars that would threaten to lift him from the ground in high winds. His trousers were in cream with a gigantic waistband, there was four vertical buttons fastened to keep them up, and the width at the bottom was over 24 inches!

When he walked he looked like the ships masts on the Onedin Line, cue music, his trousers like sails beginning to unfurl, you could hear them flap wildly on a breezy evening.

"Do you need help getting down the steps, Coco?" Guy giggled.

"What? No…pffft." he threw his father a black glance.

"They new?" I asked as I stared up and down his entire outfit.

"Yeah. Cool hey? My birthday presents." he held onto the door as he struggled out, looking a little scared of the height.

When he stood next to me he was, for the first time in his 'short' life, taller than me, (apart from the time he walked on stilts for thirteen days to win a bet!).

"How you gonna play football in 'em though?" I queried.

"Easy, they feel the same as normal shoes." he explained as we began walking. "...although..erghh..I had a few blisters yesterday ... but it's worth it..ah!" his face contorting slightly with each step.

Apparently they had a negative effect on the flexibility of his knees as well, as they didn't appear to be working at all now. His legs were ramrod straight and stiff. I think the six inch heels were hollow too because it sounded like he was walking on coconut shells at times. If I closed my eyes I could imagine being accompanied by a Shire horse as we walked. He fished in his pocket, and pulled out a pair of black leather, women's gloves. He passed one to me and began pulling his onto the right hand, glancing up at me in between his tugging.

"Put it on ... go on." he nodded at the glove in my hand.

"It's a girl's glove!"

"I know that, don't I? I was the one that nicked them off my mother ... idiot!" he flexed all his fingers, stretching the soft leather to fit.

I pulled the glove on, there was felt inside and when I got it on it came just above my wrist. Really not a good look.

"Are we the 'Black Hand Gang' again, or is it Black Power? Like at the Olympics, Tommy Smith, I raised my gloved fist up and lowered my head ... so iconic ... so memorable ... so not a Caucasian look! The athletes, by the way, readers, looked wonderful. Me? Not so much, I just looked a little bonkers as usual.

"Who? Tommy Smith? The fat Liverpool footballer with the drinker's nose? He never wore a black glove at the Olympics!! For a moment he nearly dared to take his eyes off the pavement that lay ahead to look at me, but thought better of it, if he tripped he was falling an awful long way!

"No Stew. The black runner, you know, the U.S. national anthem...hmm?" I recreated the stance again.

"Do you realise how stupid you look? Really stupid!" he shook his head as we walked on towards Douglas Street.

In the middle of the street ahead of us were three boys, kicking a football between them, Geoff, Digger and Gary. Two smaller boys, Dave and Olly, sat on the kerb exchanging football cards, and on the pavement were three girls playing hopscotch. Debbie was hopping onto the number five as Paula and Denise looked on, a skipping rope and two bald tennis balls lay discarded on the floor by their feet.

The noise of laughter drifted on the summer breeze, and I smiled broadly as my name was called out and a hail of hands raised to me and Stew. They were all were wearing one black glove. Apart from Digger who had a purple one on his right hand. Had I missed something?

"What is it then?" I turned and quizzed Stew again waving my glove in front of his face.

He ignored me and concentrated on the football that was coming our way, it bounced on the road up towards his chest, he controlled it and it fell to his feet. He pulled back his right leg like the Tin Man from Oz, stiff and straight, and launched a huge kick … the ball flew sideways and hit Paula on the side of the head and dropped into football cards Dave was holding … Alex Stepney and Mike Channon were knocked flying! Stew muttered 'hat-trick!'

"Arghhhh…" Paula turned and stared daggers at me and Stew. Stew, stood just behind me, pointed at my head and grimaced.

"Hammy … you stupid, ugly … git!" she screamed at me, laughter erupted from all around, "It's not funny … that really hurt!" she rubbed her beetroot coloured ear to prove it.

"Hey, it wasn't me, it was Stew." I claimed my innocence immediately.

"Shut it, you div!" she turned and let Denise check that her brains hadn't been knocked out of the opposite ear.

I turned to a smiling Stew, and demanded he told her, he ignored me and continued into the small circle of footballers. I stared at his back, then at Paula who mouthed an obscenity and stuck two fingers up at me … a female Kes!

I walked up to the gang, who one by one pushed me, one to the other. Digger tried but really didn't carry the weight, but because I didn't want to hurt his feelings I pretended to be knocked sideways … that's been my life … always pushed about way too easily by.

"Gloves boys, why are we wearing one black glove?" I demanded once I had regained my balance.

Geoff turned and gave me a deep, lingering … if not smouldering look and began singing!

"Coo..coo..I just want you…

182

"I really love the things that you do..(He raised his gloved hand and pointed his index finger at me, walking slowly towards me)

"Come on, love-a me too..(then everybody pointed at my smiling face, curling their fingers as they pointed..then they all sang together)

"WON'T YOU BE MY COO CA CHOOOOooooooooooo?"

"Alvin, flipping, Stardust? He wasn't number one on Top of the Pops, was he?" I giggled as the gang surrounded me, all serenading me.

"Tom Cat, you know where it's at ... won't you come back to my flat?" they continue to sing as the memory fades slowly to black. Over the singing my giggling can be heard slipping away as the subtitles roll ... ah this is The Life of Bri.

WAITING FOR GORDO

The lightest of sky blue skies had claimed squatting rights over my Moston home during the Easter holidays. The wind and rain of the previous week had been well and truly evicted, it was time to be out of the house.

Me, Stew and my faithful hound, Trumper, trudged intently along Rudd Street towards the Diggy.

School was out, and we both were determined to make the most of our holiday. We were both wearing vegetable sieves on our heads, mine was too small and looked like a metal pork pie hat with a handle sticking out at an angle, whilst Stews was enormous and looked like something an eccentric woman may wear to impress at Royal Ascot on a Lady's Day. As we walked his headwear would fall to one side, he would attempt to rebalance it, then it would drop down on the other, as a helmet for a Knight of the Round Table, it was hilariously useless.

We both carried wooden swords we had nailed together from some dumped garden fencing we had found on the tip. We had taken the fencing back to Lakin Street and used Stews dads saw, hammer and a few rusty nails to create a couple of timber Excalibur's.

Stew had borrowed a roasting tin from his mother's kitchen, and, with the help of the hammer and chisel, he had managed to turn it into a semi-believable shield. He had bashed two holes into the side panels and ran one of his dad's good belts through them, this was his handle.

"I wish this flaming helmet would stay straight." Stew moaned as his right hand, holding his sword, attempted to rebalance the stainless steel sieve.

"You should have got a tea towel too and put that on your head and let the helmet sit on that." I suggested.

"Yeah, hey, I might take me jumper off and put that under it!"

We walked on jauntily, heading for a derelict patch of ground just to the rear of Spreadbury Street. It ran the length of the ginnel that ran from Rudd Street to Brendon Avenue, and about half the width of a football pitch. It had large, overgrown privet hedges up to twenty foot high, which ran down the ginnel side and a lot of different shaped garages separating it from the Diggy. The ground was green with grasses that rose up to my chest, (Stewarts chin!) and it provided a playground of countless options, from jungles for Tarzan to Sherwood Forest for Robin Hood. Today it was to play host to a couple of Knights of the Round Table.

We ploughed through the dense foliage towards our den, this was a selection of wooden doors we had found on the tip. There were seven altogether, four that created the walls and three lay across the top to make a roof. Discarded linoleum had been spread over the top as a waterproofing material, and odd pieces of carpet laid as flooring inside.

An old red settee was placed at the rear and even though you could were only able to lay flat on it because of the restrictive height of the ceiling, it was always the prime spot for any member of our gang.

Trumper followed slowly, lost in the grass to my rear. I could hear his plodding paws close behind.

"Nearly there, I bags the couch." I cried from behind Stew.

"You're bagging nothing, it's finders keepers rule today." he started a slow jog that caused his 'helmet' to slide backwards off his head.

"Hey, I bags'd it! You can't say finders keepers … it's not lost!"

"Wohh!" Stew stopped suddenly causing me to run into his back and drop my sword.

"Whatcha doin…?" Stew turned his head to the side and put his finger to his lips suggesting I shut up.

"There's someone in our den!" he whispered angrily.

"It'll just Digger or Geoff Marsden." I suggested as Stew peered through the small entrance.

"No, it's a man … and he's asleep."

"A man?"

"I think it's a tramp. Right, send Trumper in to attack him." he said, he was kneeling now like an army officer.

"Only thing Trumper'll attack is his dinner, he may lick him to death if you want?"

"What's the point of a dog that can't rip someone's throat out?" he asked, it had always rankled with Stew that I hadn't let him train my pet into an attack dog. "Useless!"

"He's not useless, he's just ...well ... nice, and there's nothing wrong with that." I argued.

"Hello ... is there somebody outside?" a very posh voice came from within our den.

"Yeah, whatcha doin' in there mister, that's our den." Stew asked with false bravado.

A face began emerging through the small gap.

"Hellooo. What have we here? Two Knights and one steed, are you here to take back your castle, good knights?" again in that clipped accent, a voice that didn't belong in those clothes.

"We are mister, and this is our den." Stew declared.

"Forsoothes, please beg my pardon for the intrusion, I shall vacate immediately." he came out on all fours, a bowler hat in his left hand.

He unfurled a body that was lean and tall, revealed a bushy, unkempt bearded face that had warm, smiling eyes. His clothes were worn and speckles of mud had dried on his trousers below the knee. They may have been dirty but they weren't torn or shabby, he had a once white shirt with a bow tie that had polka dots upon it and a grey plain jumper that had a string of wool pulled loose at the bottom on the left. He tugged the jacket straight, then the jumper, finally popping his hat on his head and tapping it down.

"Well, boys, are you going to introduce yourselves before you run me through with your magnificent swords? You are Sir....?" he put his hand out to me.

"Er.." I looked at Stew, who just shrugged. "I'm Brivanhoe!" I didn't shake his hand.

"Brivanhoe! Excellent ... and you Sir Knight are?" he turned to Stew.

"I'm Sir Stewpotalot!" he grinned with pride at the name he had given himself.

"Ahhh, Sir Stewpot..alot...mmm ... a name that runs a shiver right down my spine." he smiled. Stew grinned weakly with just his thin lips.

"Are you a tramp, mister?" Stew asked loudly and tactlessly.

"A tramp!" he said with indignation. "I, good sir, am a gentleman of the road ... an Earl of the highway ... a Knight of the boulevard." he said this then bowed, removing his hat with right hand and sweeping it down in front of him as he did,

"Ain't that just other names for tramps?"

"No, Sir Stewpottlealottle, it isn't! I am a gentleman who has fallen, a long way, admittedly, but once I hit the bottom I shall bounce back, and once I rebound off the floor I intend to soar once again, like a kite in a high wind." he explained.

"It's ... alot, like Lance ... alot, not ottle, like..er.. Lance a bottle." Stew said with a frown, feeling he was being ribbed.

"I apologise, I have a short term memory problem due to the lack of regular sustenance." he rubbed his stomach with his left hand as he replaced his hat on his head.

188

"Is that some sort of medicine, mister?" I queried.

"Sustenance? No, no ... it's food, my boy, something to raise my blood sugar, and please call me Gordo, for we are now acquaintances, are we not?" he smiled.

"I don't know! What's an acwinnatence ... ackawintenance ... what's one of them, erm ... Gordo? I stuttered.

"Erm well ... it is not quite friends ... but we now know each other's names. Do you compre...erm...understand, Brivanhoe?" he gave a winning smile.

"Yep. Think so." I didn't!

"Jolly good. If I had a bite to eat, I could head out in the safe knowledge I wouldn't faint on my journey." he looked at me and then slowly turned to Stew.

"Do you want us to get you some grub, mister...erm...Gordo?" Stew asked.

"A piece of dry bread, a smidgen of leaves from your mother's tea caddy so I can make a nice hot cup of tea, now that would be marvellous boys."

"I can't bring a kettle, Gordo, mum'll go potty." Stew said.

"No, no, I have a little canteen. If you could just bring a bottle of water and some tea leaves, and I will make a little fire here." he pointed down to the flattened space in front of the dens entrance.

"A fire...great, we'll go and get some bread and see what else we can get too." I cried. "I love fires!"

"Back soon…" we both turned on our heels and fled, homeward, Trumper following close behind.

"Ahhh..he that is thy friend indeed, he will help thee in thy need … go boys, fly like the wind." he called after us.

"Okay, Gordo, you get the fire going. See you soon." Stew yelled back.

*

We returned 20 minutes later, as we turned up the back entry, the smell of burning wood and smoke was in the air. In our arms was a selection of goodies. Stew had two milk bottles, one with milk and the other filled with water. He also had half a loaf of Sunblest. I was carrying bread too, some butter, three triangles of cheese and an egg. Trumper walked at my side, staring up at the food.

"Gordo, we're back." Stew called out when we were about twenty feet away, the den was below the grass height and was hidden from view, but the small curling spiral of blue-grey smoke gave away our destination.

"My two Knights return from their quest laden down with rations that would make King Arthur's mouth moisten. Well done friends, we will eat like Royalty ourselves." he said in his deep voice.

We smiled at his lavish greeting, and offered up the food, he stared intently at each item before taking each one and placing them on the floor near the fire.

"Tea? Were we unlucky with our quest for tea?" disappointment edging into his tone.

"Nope" Stew dug into his pocket and pulled out a small packet of PG Tips, he raised it up to head height and swung it like a pendulum, smiling theatrically.

"Ahhh, Sir Stewpotalot, if you weren't already knighted, I would tap your shoulders with a sword, myself, right now." his disappointment had evaporated. "Twigs, boys, fetch some long dry twigs." he demanded.

"But the fires already going." I said, pointing at the crackling blaze in front of us.

"We need them as toasting forks, to prod onto the bread, make our toast without roasting our fingers." he was now pouring the water into a smoke blackened, metal pot. We turned and started our search immediately.

Gordo placed the pot onto a flat rock at the edge of the fire, house bricks surrounded the flames, stopping it from spreading. He then pulled a tin cup out of an old rucksack, the cup was covered in bumps and dents and he placed it to the side near the pot. The butter was unwrapped to reveal its deep yellow colour, but kept from the heat to try and stop it melting as it was already incredibly soft from the warm weather.

We returned with about eight sticks each, they were dropped at the chef's feet. He perused them, then bending down he picked up, one by one, the sticks that had failed his examination. These were unceremoniously thrown on the fire, three were left, these were placed at 3, 6 and 9 O'clock positions round the fire, Gordo had laid large flat stones while we were gone, and these were to be our seats.

The water eventually came to a rolling boil and he poured it carefully over the tea leaves and left it to brew, the bread meanwhile was slowly toasted on the twigs, then buttered, the triangles of cheese were shared equally and for a while the talking took a back seat while we ate our food. Trumper was rewarded for his patience with a round of toast, unbuttered. Not his food of choice, but beggars cannot be choosers.

Once we were fed, we all agreed it was a banquet worthy of the highest nobility in the land.

Half an hour later, Stew was lay on the ground, a long piece of grass was in his mouth and it wobbled first left then right as he lazily chewed on it, Trumper had his head across his chest and was having his ear scratched by Stewart's fingers...everybody was happy.

We had permitted Gordo to remove one of the doors from the roof, this allowed him to sit upright on the red sofa, his head protruding above the rest of the roofline of the den. It looked like he was sat in a 1920's airplane that lacked wings, or an enormous sidecar that had lost its motorcycle.

"What's your real name, Gordo?" I quizzed.

"Ahh, I was, and suppose I still am, Gordon Seymour."

"What was you before you was a tramp?"

"Oooh, not a tramp dear boy, please. I was an actor, I trod the boards, darling." he raised his eyes skyward.

"An actor!! Have you been in Z Cars, or Doctor Who?" I asked excitedly.

"I have...both actually...small parts mind, but I've always been more theatre than television."

"Woh, Doctor Who..crikey, really?"

"Yes, but I was dressed as some alien, and had two lines to perform...nothing to write home about."

"I would write home, I'd write to me Nana too...and Stew, I'd send him a letter that said 'hey, big head, watch me on Saturday'...he would be dead jealous." Stew mumbled that he would be.

"Yes, I dare say, but like I said, theatre is my real love, I have done lots of plays, have you ever heard of 'Cat on a Hot Tin Roof?'..." he asked.

"Yes, we call it dancing cat!" Stew laughed.

"Why would you call it that?"

"Cos, when you get the corrugated roofing really hot on the fire..." he pointed at the flames on our campfire, "... you then chuck a cat on it...and it dances, jumps around like mad!" he explained to an open mouthed Gordo.

"Not the 'Cat on a Hot Tin Roof' I was thinking about, to be honest...." he said with a really slow shake of his head, his eyes never leaving Stews. I butted in, desperate to change the tack.

"Mine and Stew's class are going to the BBC...to be on telly next month, it's called 'We Want to Sing,' and The Spinners and Sandie Shaw are going to on it." I said.

"Ohhh, Sandie. Now there's a lovely girl, I was the one who suggested she take her shoes off, you know?" he said, finally breaking Stew's stare.

"Mum does that with me...was she making a mess of your carpet? She shouldn't be walking in people's houses with dirty shoes on." I consoled.

"Noooo, she shouldn't'." he smiled softly.

"What else have you been in?" I asked.

"In the theatre, I've done Room at the Top..." he looked at both of us hoping for a nod of recognition.

"Nope." I shook my head showing I'd never heard of it.

"Err...I've done lots of Shakespeare ... do you know any the Bard?" he asked.

"Don't know the Bard bloke, but Mum likes Shayspeare. She read me one the other week ... 'rough winds do shake me, my darling, May'." I grinned broadly with pride.

"That ... that is magnificent. I have played both Hamlet and Romeo." he continued.

"Hey, that's Hammy's name!" Stew piped up from ground level.

"Hammy? Who is this Hammy?" Gordo asked bemused by Stews input.

"Me, I'm Hammy, Hammy Hamblett, that's me name."

"You are called Hamlet, how ironic! I have played him ... and yet, here you are lucky enough to live it, my young Prince of Denmark." he laughed out loud.

"I know, 'snot spelt the same though. Mines got a B in it."

"To B or not to B ... that is the question, Brivanhoe..ha ha."

"Ha, good one, Gordo" Stewart shouted up.

194

"So why aren't you acting now?" I asked quietly, lowering my head in case he told me to mind my own business.

"I messed up. I froze." he looked up at the blue sky, and puffed out his cheeks, the air was released very, very slowly.

"In a freezer, or in the Arctic or summat?"

"On the stage, lad, I wish I had been at North Pole." his head was still back, lay on the back of the sofa.

"Had someone left the door open?" I was lost why he had been so cold.

"No, no ... it's a long story. I was understudy to an actor, it was in a big, big play in London ... and the irony does not stop ... for it was Camelot..." he straightened up and flung his arms wide, indicating the den and our surroundings were Camelot.

"Oh flipping eck, London!" I said, still a little lost. Stew sat up now, his hands on the ground behind him.

"Flipping heck, indeed. The lead actor was taken ill and I had to go on stage, people had paid a lot of money to see Dickey ... and there was me ... I blew a fuse. I could not for the life of me remember any lines..." his head dropped in shame.

"You forgot the words!!?" I exclaimed.

"I did. Like I said, I froze ... I just stood there for what seemed like eternity. Eventually I was prompted and we staggered through, but it was a disaster. I was booed...people were leaving the theatre halfway through..." he stopped and let his hands cover his face.

"Did they sack you?" I whispered.

195

"Oh yes, and that was my career in tatters … nobody would touch me with a barge pole after that."

"Why did they want to see your willy?" Stew asked looking confused.

"My willy?" Gordo was taken aback.

"You said they wanted to see your 'dickey'!" he said innocently.

"They wanted to see Dickey … Dickey Burton. Richard Burton … the actor, not my genitalia, my dear boy!"

"He's married to someone famous, isn't he?"

"He is, although he is famous for more than his marriage, he is the most wonderfully, talented actorrr" his r rolled like a boulder pushed off the side of Snowdon.

"So you're a rubbish actor, then?"

"Stewpottle, I am lower than rubbish!" he answered this slowly, looking back at Stew.

"You must have been good to have been given the substitute's shirt, they wouldn't give that spot to a rubbish actor, that'd be stupid." I reasoned.

"Ha..thank you, Brian … I suppose I did have a smattering of talent, but that is all lost in the mists of time, tainted forever by that one night of disaster."

"Well, why not do some acting for us. Show us some Shayspeare, let's see how good you are." I suggested brightly.

"...or how bad you are!!" we both turned and looked at Stew. "....whaaaat? I'm just sayin'!"

"What? Here? I don't … Shakespeare? Ha ha … okay, let's see how bad I am then, hey boys?" he looked around the grassy waste ground. "I will do the Hamlet soliloquy, 'to be, or not to be' … have you heard of it?"

"Yeah, to be or not to be, that is the question...he he." I replied with the little I knew. Gordo finally crawled out of the den on all fours.

"Well done, Prince. I'm going to be doing Hamlet for Hamblett … how surreal this day is turning out to be." he began removing his jacket. Then he dropped his hands by his side and waggled them as if to loosen the muscles. Then his whole face changed, a more sorrowful look … his eyes looked out up and beyond where me and Stew sat, cross legged, Stew still stroking Trumpers head. Then, with a voice deep and resonant that vibrated on our rib cages he began.

"To be….or not to be. That is the question.

Whether 'tis nobler in the mind to suffer the slings and arrows

of outrageous fortune, or take arms against a sea of troubles.." he was suddenly lost in the moment, his demeanour transformed, his audience of three gazed at this man and watched him grow large and imposing, he was performing a 16th century soliloquy and no Thunderbirds episode would ever hold us this entranced. Both our mouths were slightly agape, our eyes wide, followed him as he strode from one side of the flattened grass in front of the den to the other, his hands emphasising certain points in the speech. It was mesmerising.

"...soft you now. The fair Ophelia? Nymph. In thy Orisons be all my sins remembered." he spoke the last two sentences gently, struggling to keep the rhythm that had made the speech wash over us, he was almost at a whisper, like he was remembering the imaginary sins that he had so obviously laid heavy upon his own shoulders, and had carried for so long. There was ten seconds of silence … then...

"Yaaay. Flipping 'eck Gordo … that was brilliant…" I cried out.

"Yeah...I didn't understand a word you said, but it still was dead good." Stew's exclamation of praise making Gordo smile broadly as he bowed continuously.

"I thank you. This beats any performance at the Globe itself. I feel a tad emotional, now!" he turned his back on us and lifted his right hand to his eyes, he shoulders heaved gently for a second or two.

"Is he crying?" I whispered to Stew.

"I think he is … what's that all about?" he muttered back.

"Don't know, I thought he'd enjoyed it!"

"What should we do? Should I pat his back…?" Stew suggested quietly as he stood.

"Er..no..." I answered, Gordo raised his right arm high, waving his hand.

"It's fine boys … I'm alright, it's just been a while since I've had reason to do..." he turned and swept his hand across in front of him. "...this"

"Well, it was really cool." I said trying to console him.

"Thank you … both of you, so, so much." he gave me and Stew a solo applause.

"Can you do the bit from Doctor Who now?" Stew asked.

"I told you, I only had two lines!" he said doubting we could be bothered to hear them.

"Yeah, but it was on Doctor Who! Which one was it?" I queried.

"It was called 'The Dimensions of Time,' I was a Morok guard who has been given the task of putting Bill in a cell."

"Bill?" Stew wondered out loud.

"....Hartnell, the Doctor, William to you, dear boys." he laughed.

"Was he the white haired Doctor?" Stew asked.

"Yes, lovely man, he liked his sauce though...ha ha...but a very nice man."

"I like my sauce, especially on burger and chips!" I offered up.

"Yes, I bet you do...Bill liked his sauce with everything...ha ha ha..." he informed us without elucidating. "..lots and lots of sauce."

"So..what did you say?"

"When?"

"To the Doctor."

"Ahh...let me see...here." he put his hand out to me, "...you be the Doctor, I'm leading you to the cell. I have my hand on your shoulder, then you say to me ... 'you are a fool, you are all in imminent danger,' I look at you and say, 'you are in more danger, believe me.' Then the Doctor..that's you, Brian..turns and says 'I understand you are scared, but fear makes companions of all of us!' then I throw the Doctor in the cell and push my

199

face up to the bars and say...'I am not scared … we have never felt this thing you call fear.' You then walk up to the bars and say.. 'Fear will be introducing itself, dear boy, and quite soon.' We then cut to another scene." he smiled at remembering so much.

"Flamin' Nora, can we act it out? Pleeease." Stew begged.

"Yes, if you want, why not? Brian first?" I nodded enthusiastically, he crawled over and whispered the words in my ear. "Now, will you remember them?" he nodded in encouragement.

"I'll try..he he." I giggled.

"Improvise if you can't...use your greatest gift, boy ... your imagination ... let's go"

I was led by my Morok guard, who I informed was an idiot and in 'eminent' danger. Gordo smiled and gave his line in perfect tone, to which I replied.

"Yes, you are scared Mister, you are actually frikened to death … and if you're not … well, you're flippin really stupid."

Gordo looked at me and then pushed me gently into the den, where, I crawled to the back and then stood through the roofless part and stared at him with the biggest grin as he answered me.

"I am not..er..frikened to death...I have never felt this thing you call frike." he acted his part wonderfully.

"Well, matey … it's here … and it's gonna batter your head in!" I declared with as much threat as a young boy could muster.

Gordo, turned and walked away. Stew clapped like a half-wit, adding a wolf whistle too.

"My turn, my turn!" he shouted.

Well done, Brian, you were magnificent. Stewart, do you remember the lines?"

"Yeah, can I have a grenade and blow you up as you try to walk away?" he really bought into the improvisation.

"Methinks your blood runs a little darker than most other boys, doesn't it Stewart?" he said with a frown.

"I don't know, should I cut meself and see?" he offered all too easily.

"No, no, it's fine, we'll take it as read...ha ha...red...no...the blood?" he looked at each of us but it went flying, high above our heads. "Never mind … erm … right, here … front and centre." I sat while Stew went through the same scene. Stew insisted he was going to pull the guards head off, pop his eyes out and use them as a table tennis balls … and finally told him that his body would be eaten by a kazillion maggots. Being honest, Gordo looked a little shaken by how much Stew was able to invest into the threat of decapitation … this was method acting at its best!

Once we had done, we relaxed around the embers of the fire. Even though the day was warm, the smell of smoke and the colours of the ash and burnt wood, glowing was hypnotic, especially to two young boys.

"Why don't you just go back to live with your mum and dad?" I suddenly asked out of the blue.

Gordo was lay on his side, his head resting on one hand, he looked up and stared at me, not with malice, more gently, like he was pondering his reply.

"I don't know, maybe because I feel I let them down. Father never wanted me to be an actor. He really wanted me to be a barrister." he said quietly.

"What...your dad wanted you to be a bannister!!!" Stew exclaimed.

"A...barristerrrr!" he annunciated perfectly so Stew heard every letter. "It's a type of lawyer ... he was one and wanted me to follow him in law." he explained further.

"Thought your dad was mad wanting you to be a bannister!" Stew smiled.

"Well..." Gordo left the sentence in the smoky air for a second..his eyes rolled slightly. "...out of the mouths of babes."

"Yeah..well ... I would go back to my mum and dad. They would look after me, they would make sure I had a bed to sleep in. Wouldn't you go back too, Stew?" I asked, Stew looked doubtful.

"I dunno, my dad keeps saying they're gonna move house while I'm at school. He said he's had enough of me, and that I drive 'em both up the wall...annnnnd...to be honest, I quite like the idea of being a tramp!" he grinned as he said the final part of his answer.

"Stewart, a life on the road is no fun, believe me." Gordo said.

"Go home, Gordo." I interceded, "I bet your mum and dad are dead worried about you." I stood up and walked about, taking care not to stand on Trumpers tail or Stewarts fingers, "Just turn up, smile, and say you need help." I implored.

"Ha.." he took a deep breath, "..you should be a counsellor, Mr. Hamblett, but it's really not that simple ... sadly."

"Why? A mum and dad, their house ... your old bed and I bet your mum'd make you sausage and chips ... with sauce too!!" I tried to paint as pretty a picture as possible.

"Ha, kill the fatted calf ... the prodigal son is home! ha ha." he scoffed,

"You can't call your mum that, she just gonna slam the door in your face!" Stew advised. "Mums really don't like being called fat anything." he looked at me for back up, I nodded, it was true.

"You two are so wise, maybe you are just what I needed. I will sleep on it tonight, I promise you, boys."

"Well, you said after you hit the bottom you'd bounce back up and fly again ... maybe me and Stew are your trampoline, and maybe you just need to flap your arms now, maybe, if you tried harder and went to your mum and dad they would get you flying up dead high again. I'd hate not having me mum and dad there, cos they're like a safety net, aren't they ... they'll always catch me if I fall. Mum picks me up, checks my knees puts a bit of spit on her hankies and rubs anything that hurts, better." I puffed out my cheeks and let out a big exhale. "...just sayin', that's all." I sat down again.

"Yeah, why is spit good for cuts? I've never understood that!" Stew asked me, I just shook my head, I never really knew how saliva worked medicinally.

Gordo looked at me, he sat up, then pushed himself to standing, a small groan let out indicated his joints were aching from being lay in one position for a while. He held his arms out to me.

"Here," he waited patiently for me to arrive for the hug, "Stewart … come on." Stew was quicker and the group hug took place.

"...and if I'm being totally honest, you really could do with a bath!" Stew said undiplomatically … his head held near Gordo's armpit … the hug ended immediately.

"I really am going to sleep on your advice boys. The bathing will be difficult, but the bouncing upwards … maybe that's a possibility. I must admit, I have felt a little more serene over the last few days and maybe you two have been sent to show me that I have served my penance. God works in mysterious ways." he smiled, then sat again, cross legged.

"Well that's the first time I've been called an angel!" Stew exclaimed.

"He didn't call us angels." I disagreed.

"He did, he said God worked in mysterious ways … and he said we had been sent … God sends angels, doesn't he Gordo?" he argued.

"Absolutely! You are both angels … and Knights of the highest order … and, even more importantly, true friends, and I thank you both."

"What for, telling you that you're still a good actor? Or for telling you to go back home to your mum?" I wondered out loud.

"For just being here, boy's....it's been a long time since I have felt so relaxed...and, to be honest, normal again.

"Yeah, I feel un-normal a lot, I know what you mean!" said Stew.

"Why does that not surprise me, Stew?" he laughed.

"I don't know!" Stew answered, "Maybe, you're hard to surprise?" he asked.

"Maybe I am...but I have been surprised today, surprised enough to take wing again..ha ha."

"Hey, I have to get back...mum said if I'm not too late I can help her with the fairy cakes."

"Fairy cakes!!" Stew exclaimed.

"What? Mum lets me lick the bowl, and there's trifle to make...Nana, and me aunties are all coming round." I explained.

"Fairy cakes … you really are a wuss!" Stew stated.

"Hey, Stewart, there is nothing wrong with helping your mother, whatever the task … baking is probably one of the nicer things you can do … the most important girl that you will ever have in your life … cherish her, make her smile, take time to enjoy her and these moments. These are your halcyon days, boys … they do not last … nothing ever lasts, apart from the love of your mother." he defended me with a passion.

"See, you still love your mum, Gordo, and she will still love you. And Stew, I don't care if you think I'm a wuss … I love cake … and I love me mum, so there. I'm off home, come on Trumper, are you coming Stew?"

"'Suspose' so. Will you be okay on your own, Gordo?" he asked our bearded friend.

"Been alone a long time now, my little friend. I am sure I will survive, worry not."

"Okidoki … come on then Hammy, see if you can sneak some cake out later."

"Might not come out, Nana's bringing down me comics, the Topper, Beezer, Dandy and Beano. That's a lot of reading." I explained as I sorted myself out, brushing grass off my shorts. "Right, Gordo, see you tomorrow, hey?"

"If you don't mind me staying in Camelot one more night?"

"Nope, our den is your den, matey … isn't it Stew?"

"Yeah, long as you don't have a wee in there … no number one's and deffo no number two's!!" he said in all seriousness.

"Well, that's a deal, worry not."

"Deal" I said, "Are you coming or not?" Stew nodded and we headed slowly towards Rudd Street. "Taraaa." we waved at our unkempt friend, he waved back then we turned and trampled through the deep grass.

Stew was knocking at my door about 11 O'clock the next morning, I was still in my pajamas, in the kitchen when mum shouted me to tell me he was there. I glugged back my milk, leaving a large white moustache across my top lip, and dropped down from my chair to the icy cold linoleum. In four seconds I was craning my head round my mum's torso at the front door, careful not to reveal my pajamas.

"Hello, whatcha want?" I enquired.

"Are you coming out, or what?"

"I need to get dressed yet."

"....and clean your teeth!" mum added from behind me.

"..and clean my teeth." I looked from Stew to mum with eyes that said 'really?' In front of my friend!

"I'll meet you on the Diggy, at the den ... hurry up, alright?"

"Yeah, see you in a bit." I said pushing the door closed in his face.

I raced past mum, into the kitchen then a sharp right turn onto the stairs. I used both hands and feet to clamber up to my room, the stairs really were that steep. Mum shouted after me to slow down, but I was already kicking off my 'jimmy' bottoms and in the middle of unbuttoning the jacket when I heard her. Shorts, tee-shirt and socks were on in record time, I lunged out of my room and virtually fell downstairs, the decibel level from my feet on would have had your average rock club shut down, my hands suffered friction burns from wallpaper and bannister.

"Going out...!" I called out as I flashed through the living room.

"Have you......?"

"Yes..." I answered the unasked question as I pulled the front door closed behind me.

The sky had been painted a translucent blue again, there was the merest sharp hint of white cloud high in the stratosphere. It appeared God had used a cut throat razor to tear open this cerulean ceiling. I raced, attempting to leap from pavement to pavement where the ginnel flooded out separating them ... always falling a foot or more short ... Bob Beamon and his gold medal slept easily in his bed. I was soon joined by my panting dog who caught me easily, after mum had obviously let him out.

When I turned into Spreadbury Street's ginnel, the cobbles made me slow. I then smelt the smoky air, Gordo had obviously had set a camp fire again.

I stepped up off the cobbles and into the deep grass between the large, out of control privets, and like a big game hunter, strode carefully through the chest high savannah. Ahead I could see Stew and Gordo, and when he spotted me he hailed a large hullo.

"Both my knights have returned, wonderful." he exclaimed.

I moved quicker when I found a path of flattened grass and was soon by the smoking embers and my pals.

"What's this?" I lifted a paper bag.

"I've brought Gordo some stuff." Stew said, a piece of half burnt toast heading to his mouth.

I opened the bag carefully, it could've been a snake, a box of spiders or his slug collection in there...but no, there was some shoes and some clothes.

"What's this?"

"It's a suit and some shoes, look at Gordo's...." he left the sentence hanging while we all stared at his mud filmed and creased footwear.

"A suit?" I asked with incredulity...""...have you nicked it?"

"No," he stared daggers at me. "It's me dad's, well, was ... but he hates it. He said to my mum at Christmas, I hate putting this thing on ... so, I thought, why not give it Gordo and dad won't ever have to wear it again! It's what my dad calls a win win situation!" he looked at me then Gordo.

"I really shouldn't Stew." he said weakly.

"No ... you should, 'cos you need it and me dad really hates it ... win ... win!" he spread his hands to show it was just karma.

"Well, I'll try it on and if you give me your address, I will send it back tout suite." he nodded, almost as much to himself as to Stew.

"Well, you can, but me dad'll probably be disappointed to see it again, to be honest.

"Can I have this last piece of bread, Gordo, do some toast?" I asked interrupting the conversation.

"You can, but I have no butter left." he replied.

I pronged the bread and sidled up to the hot embers, Trumper watching carefully. I wasn't hungry but making toast outside was a joy ... even if it was inedible.

Gordo bent and entered the wooden den, bag in hand.

"Your dad'll go mad, you do know that don't you?" I said in a low voice without looking up from my steaming bread.

"He won't even realise its gone 'til Christmas, then he'll just think it's in the cleaners or something … he's not gonna think I've nicked a suit, is he?" he tried to reason away.

"His suit is missing … he's gonna think, now, where can it be? Then he's gonna think … Stewart!!!" I pointed at him as I said his name.

"Well, Gordo said he's posting it back!" Stewart launched a rock he'd been holding towards the garages, creating a large bang as it hit the asbestos roof and rumbled down and off.

"Again, he's gonna think…where has it been? Why is my suit being posted back to me? Stewart!" I pointed at him as I said his name again, I then had a little giggle at my logic, anything wrong in the Neale household … Stewart!

"Well boys?" we both turned to see Gordo looking rather dapper, it was like the suit had been made for him, a simple dark blue. Apart from the scruffy beard, a shirt in that was desperately in need of a bin and the dark, baggy eyes of a man who'd awoken in a ramshackle, children's lean-to, housing project, you might not put him in the tramp category.

"You don't look as scruffy!" Stew said succinctly.

"High praise indeed from such a sartorial beggar as you!" he laughed out loud. "The trousers are a little tight around the 'undercarriage', but I think I'll survive." he shook his left leg as if to gain a little more room in there.

"You still need a shave, though. Then you'll look even better." I added my voice.

"Well..." he rubbed his facial hair. "...I'd need a razor and some soap."

"I'll go and nick my dad's." Stew offered immediately.

"You know? I suspected you might suggest that, Stewart ... ha ha." Gordo said. "...scissors too if possible, I need to trim it down first. I cannot believe I'm encouraging this. I really should not be putting you in this compromising position."

"It's all right, he's had a shave already, and I can take it back after you have ... Hammy, your toast!" he'd cut in to stop my bread bursting into flames. "...erm...yeah, I can take it back as soon as you are done." he continued while I shook my charcoaled toast frantically, a blue smoke shield being created in front of me.

Trumper had raised himself from the ground now and sat on his haunches suspecting that food, inedible to most humans, was about to be discarded ... although it is difficult to read a dog's expression, it was obvious he was not happy when I began scratching, with my fingernails at the blackened surface of the bread, I was determined to bring this toast back from the dead ... Lazarus style, at least he had the joy of black snow falling onto his face and lapping tongue.

Once I had burnt the rear side of my bread too, bitten into it like a charcoal Ryvita, and then instantly discarded it ... (much to my dog's delight). We headed off to Stew's at a sprint. Returning in no time we sat and

211

watched intently as this new friend, slowly and carefully pulled and trimmed his beard, then soaping the remains with the canister of foam from Stew's dad's shaving paraphernalia. His swipes were not as smooth as my fathers, he was constantly having to unclog the blade, long hairs blocked it up … he twisted the handle and this opened up the razor and revealed the blade which he wiped on his, now redundant, trousers by his feet.

After half an hour of struggle his face began to appear from the mask of fuzz, and when he had decided no more could be done, Stew passed him a bottle of cologne … I say cologne … Hai Karate may not actually fit into that bracket but he splashed it on and although not a fragrance he had ever worn in his previous life, this scent was so much preferable to the one he had been wearing in the little time we had known him.

"Well, boy's this is as good as it gets for now … voila" his smile seemed wider, his teeth seemed whiter, he looked sixty years younger!

"Well, you are still ugly, but not as dirty." Stew said things as he saw them, I'm tempted now to think he may have had a touch of Asperger's … or just enjoyed being a tad cruel.

"Boy's it is time for me to return to the real world. I thought about your words and nipping back to my parents and asking them to be my port in this personal storm of mine may be my best bet. If I have any chance of engaging with this life again, asking them for help seems so logical now...my personal game of hide and seek is now officially over … I'm homeward bound, boys. I've allowed myself to believe you can never go back … but … you can! And sometimes going back is the hardest, but best thing to do."

"I hate going back to the dentist!" I said, agreeing with the sentiment.

"Yeah, I hate going back to school after the summer holidays … wish you didn't have to go back there." Stew added.

"Or going back home after you have got your school report...ohhh...I do like going back to bed 'tho!" Gordo just looked on in amazement … this was like verbal tennis. We took his heartfelt and slightly emotional statement and trashed it. But only because it was lost on us … the importance of his 180 degree life turn was beyond our grasp.

"...yeah, love it when you get up for school and realise it's Saturday, you jump straight back in bed..."

"With your teddy...ha ha..!" I accused Stew.

"It's not a teddy … it's a gorilla and gorilla's ain't soppy. Are they Gordo?" Stew asked, looking for an ally.

"I don't think so." exasperated at conversation. "I do not believe gorillas are girly in any sense of the word!"

"See, and he doesn't get into the bed. He just sits at the bottom, so don't start thinking I am hugging him … or that he sleeps on my pillow."

"It's just that every time I go in your room … there he is … leaning against your headboard looking like he's been kissed..he he." I was relentless.

"I do not kiss him…"

213

"Boys...boys. It's time to break camp, so let's have no arguing. Let's get Stewart's fathers shaving kit together, put the fire out and get me on the road home."

"Okay, but I don't kiss him!" Stew still in defensive mode.

Over the next twenty minutes we bagged up all the stuff that was to be returned into Stew's dad's ownership, including his patent leather shoes that had been too small for our friend.

Then it was time for him to go, so we walked with him, we took the back entry's initially, Stew was a little wary of his father seeing an unkempt chap walking with his son, bedecked in his best suit! It may have taken a little bit of explanation and a removal of a thick belt. So we walked on cobbles, me, Stew, Trumper and this man, his bag slung over his shoulder. Every minute or so he would stop, pull at the trousers that insisted on trying to hide up his backside, he would wiggle his hips, grimace, and then start walking again. Gordo was going home ... but it didn't seem it was going to be a comfortable journey.

WATER, WATER EVERYWHERE

The Sunday afternoon was hot, no, it was sultry and even when the breeze decided to grant a little relief, it was momentary and only a degree or two cooler. This was a day to do very little or even less. Two boys had ventured from Lakin Street to Broadhurst Park, they were dressed alike with grey shorts and bri-nylon tee shirts on. There was a dog in tow, the dogs tongue lolled out of a heavily breathing mouth like a dried out lettuce leaf, but in a shade of pink rather than a deep chlorophyll green.

When they arrived outside the last house before the park, Stewart, the smaller, thinner boy, sloped down the side of the house and used the tap attached to the outer kitchen wall. He refilled an empty Tizer bottle, they had drank their first ration on the ten minute walk to the park. A woman banged on the window and suggested Stew left the premises immediately. Stew tried to smile an innocent smile as he showed her the Tizer bottle.

"Go on, sod off!" she shouted through the window.

"You're a right ugly cow." Stew whispered so she couldn't hear, but the smile was still broad so she'd think he was just passing the time of day.

"Get off my land, and leave my tap alone you little scamp." she had now appeared at the side door, a flowery pinny on and brandishing a dish towel in her hand as if it was a deadly weapon.

"Calm down, missus, I'm only getting water, you don't want us to die or something, do you?"

"You're not going to bloody die, get on with you."

"There's little black kids dying in 'Baffra' because of people like you, missus. You'd let me and my friend..." he turned to find his friend had hidden from view. "...where's he gone?" he wondered out loud.

"This isn't Biafra, this is Manchester, son. People don't die of thirst in the North West of England!" she had put her hands on her hips now as she stepped out of her kitchen. Stew had begun screwing the cap back on the bottle.

"I bet there is, I bet there's kids all over Moston on the verge of death from thirst. I probably could get you arrested for killing kids. You'd go to prison 'cos you'd killed me and my mate and Trumper!" the dog was lapping at the puddle that encircled Stews scuffed shoes.

"I am not arguing with an idiot child about stupid things like murder. I am sick and tired of coming out and chasing you lot off."

"Well, don't then! Just let us get our water and you can watch Crossroads, and if you were a kind lady you could even give us some broken biscuits or bake us some cakes. We'd call you that lovely old woman next to the park rather than Witchypoo!" he shrugged his shoulders as if to inspire her to make the right choice.

"Witchypoo! Old! I'm 34, you little devil." she stepped forward causing Trumper to back away from the puddle.

"Hey, if it was me I'd wanna be liked. I wouldn't want all the kids to think I was keeping all the water for myself. Right I've got to go and find my invisible friend, see yor." with that he lifted the bottle in a farewell gesture. "Come on Trumper, let's go and see where your chicken of an owner is." he turned and ambled up the path Trumper following reluctantly.

"Old! A witch? The little beggar" the dish towel had slipped from her grasp now and lay crumpled, like her spirit, on the ground. The crime had ended up a slow motion one with the two not rushing from her premises.

"Hello Trumper," I called lazily, when he appeared from the woman's path.

"Where did you get to? I was expecting some back up from my wingman."

"I thought you had it covered yourself."

"I'd hate to go to war with you." he said with disgust. "I'd spit on your shoes if my gob wasn't so dry." he shook his head.

"What? I think she knows my mum." I tried to explain.

"Well, if she did, you should have asked her for the water. You would have said all them pleases and thank you's, rather than have me telling her she was a potential murderer."

"You didn't!"

"I bloody did. She tried to insist you can't die of thirst in Manchester."

217

"Course you can, in this weather you could die in an hour if you don't get water or Tizer." I agreed.

"Exactly, stupid cow." he hurdled the green plastic covered wire fence like an antelope.

"Well, it would serve her right if we died, you know, prove her wrong." I lifted the bottom of the fence revealing enough for Trumper to scurry under in to the park like a canine commando.

Stew was already parkside, water bottle in one hand, an egg shaped football in the other.

"Come on you scruffy mutt." he enticed, a smile on his face, not an ounce of malice in his beckoning.

"He's not a mutt..er..oh..he is really, in't he?" I decided, "But he's my mutt."

"Flippin 'eck, Hammy, the word mutt was invented for Trumper, scruffy, chunky and lazy, he is the canine version of you..haaa!" he laughed out loud.

"Bog off, I'm not a, err...what's a canine?" my argument floundering at the first obstacle.

"It's a dog, numb nuts!" he looked amazed at my lack of general knowledge.

"Is it, oh, well if I was gonna be a dog, I'd wanna be Trumper. Everybody loves him, even you do, sorta!" I said as I swung my legs, in a sweeping motion over the half collapsed fence, I paused half way and lay there, the fence had become a hammock.

"Hey I don't love him. I don't love anyone. I put up with him like I put up with you ... and because he doesn't mither us when we're playing togga, or headers." he had become defensive, not wanting to show his soft side, miniscule as it was. I fell out of my fence hammock onto the floor and jumped to my feet next to Trumper.

"Well, I do," I bent slightly and shook his head with my hand, ears and unkempt hair moving like a badly fitting toupe, "Don't I, Trumps? Who loves you, baby? I do, I loves ya!"

Trumper, unlike his scalp was unmoved, he just waited patiently, sat on his haunches, waiting to see which path we would eventually follow. Left down to the wide open spaces of the park or right, along the narrow path that ran with the fence. Stew decided ... and to the right it was.

We had to move slowly, dipping under the boughs of trees that grew up against the fence, then pushing through a couple of large leaved but dense bushes, each branch Stew passed he made sure swung back, whiplash style, hitting me about my head and chest.

"Stoppit, Stew..." just as the last twig struck me on the forehead, "ouch, are you are doing that on purpose"

"Grrrrrrr..." Trumper didn't mind a little fun with his master, but he knew when to step up and warn that enough was enough.

"Woooo. Calm down, Tiger." Stew said, laughing.

"Well done, Trumps, you tell him." I thanked him, and suddenly the clearing came into view.

One hundred square feet of flat, green grass, bordered on two sides by thick dense bushes and trees, at the back, the parks metal barred fence, all topped off by a more secure and private wooden one put up by the owner of the water tap house and her neighbours. In front of us was a view of trees on the other side of the park, a very deep dell lay between us where the light struggled to penetrate through the canopy above. Both sides of the cloughs were very steep, it was a sharp V gouged out 12,000 years previously by the retreating glacier from the last ice age.

I flopped onto the dry, hard and now yellowing grass. Trumper, circled twice before he dropped like a sack of potatoes. He had wisely chose the shade of a prickly branched bush that had small white flowers decorating it, that attracted the inhabitants of a local bee hive.

"Funny thing about Trumper is," I said, "I think he loves my mum, more than me." my head was now resting on the football.

"I think everybody likes your mum more than you, I like Hitler more than you and he wasn't nice at all?" Stew admitted as he clambered up a low hanging branch of one of the bordering trees.

"But Trumper, he's my dog. I do everything for him, but when my mum comes in, he goes really potty, gets her slipper in his mouth and his tails wagging like a helicopter blade. He makes these whining noises too. He doesn't do the same for me or my dad. Just sort of nods at us and goes back to sleep"

"Oh, you do everything for him? So you feed him?" Stew asked, now straddling the branch like a resting leopard, legs and arms hanging either side, head lay facing me, worry free.

"No, I can't undo the tins ... they're too sharp, mum says."

"Do you...erm...pick up his dog mess in the back yard?"

"Urgggghhhh. Stew, are you joking? He does some real stinkers and, God, they're big, like maffise chocolate logs" I shivered at the thought.

"Do you wash him, you know, proper like, in the bath?"

"No, I did once, but mum said I made the kitchen look like the Great Flood, and we'd need a boat to get to the back door!" I told him, slowly shaking my head gently so it didn't fall off the ball that I was using as a pillow.

"Do you let him out first thing in the morning, into the yard?"

"Noooooo Stew, mum does all the rubbish things, I just do all the good things."

"Like what?"

"I wrestle him, I scratch his belly and make his leg go crazy shaky, I let him on my bed at night, when my mum says I'm not 'sposed to, I give him sausages under the table at teatime....errr," my tongue now flicking out of my mouth to the left while my eyes stared upwards, searching in the air for other wonderful things I did for him, "Oh yeah, and I race him home, whenever me and you've been playing footie and he's allowed to come out playing with us, I do that all the time ... see, great fings, not like the rubbish fings, mum does!"

"Nope, it really doesn't make sense. If I was a dog, I think I would love someone who wrestled me,

221

much more than someone who just picked up me pooh ...
maybe Trumper's just a little bit mad, I've always
wondered why he don't like me much to be honest?" he
reasoned.

Trumper, lifted his head and stared up at Stew,
probably, just because he was speaking ... and lay up a
tree, but it looked comically like he was surprised Stew
didn't know why he kept his distance from him.

"If he is mad ... it's a nice mad, not a loony mad"
I took a heavy draught of the ever warming water, "Do
you want a drink, you nutter?" I held the bottle up
towards Trumper.

He heaved his body onto four legs and
lethargically wandered over to me, I lifted the bottle
above his head and poured the liquid into his mouth, his
tongue lapped like mad, trying to manoeuvre every last
drop down his throat. I stopped and he looked down at
the grass, hoping for a puddle, but the ground was just as
thirsty as him, if not more so.

"Mind you, Stew."

"What?"

"She is nice."

"Who?"

"Me mum."

"She's all right ... for a mum."

"Yeah ... a big softie, really."

"Oh yeah, bit like mine."

Suddenly Trumper sat up, his ears turning and
twisting like radar dishes ...it appeared someone had
plugged him into the mains.

"What is it, boy?"

"Look," Stew whispered, "...a rabbit" he pointed to the edge of the dell. A grey rabbit sat like a statue, hoping to blend in with the background. Stew had other thoughts. "Trumper, rabbits ... fetch boy, fetch." he said accentuating the 's' in rabbits.

Trumper spied the poor creature and like a whippet he leapt towards it. The rabbit turned and plunged down the hill, into the gloom.

"No, Trumper stay." I called in vain as Trumper disappeared over the ledge.

Stew swung down from the tree like a chimpanzee, and followed him downwards, I brought up the rear.

The slope was very steep and the ground made up of clay, Stewart had no problem following my barking dog, he was like a mountain goat, sure footed and agile whereas I was like Baloo the bear...better on all fours. I slid on my backside, sticks and stones finding ways up and into my shorts, my hands grabbing at tall grasses in a vain attempt to slow me.

"Can you see him?" I shouted to Stew.

"Yeah, he's on the path on the other side of the water."

I watched Stew come off the slope below me and land on the narrow gap before the tiny river and with a graceful leap land on the path opposite.

I landed like a rolling, dead buffalo, tried the leap and failed to vault the gap landing in the water that took great pleasure in filling my shoes.

"Flaming Nora!" I cried as I stepped onto the path. My shoes sloshed water out with each step, the socks hung low revealing my ankles to the world.

"You really are useless aren't you?"

"I just misjudged my jump."

"Jump? You jump like my nana, and she's 78!"

"Where's Trumper?" I asked, changing the subject.

"Here he is." in the distance Trumper appeared from around the bend in the path, something in his mouth.

"Flaming 'eck, he's only gone and caught it." Stew said ecstatically, "We can have a barbeque!" he pulled a lighter out of his pocket. "Get some sticks, Hammy."

"He's never caught anything in his life, he's too slow."

"Bags I get a leg, can I gut it? His other hand had his pen knife in it."

"Well I'm not eating anything. Here boy, have you got a rabbit, boy, have you? Trumper picked up his pace and increased his tail wag too as he approached.

I bent into a crouch to entice him into my arms and he loped faster towards me, happy to be bringing home some food.

"I could make a hat out of the skin, like Davy Crockett!" Stew mused.

"Oh you dirty dog, put it down," I cried. "It's a flamin' rat!"

"I can still gut it, but I ain't eating it, Hammy." Stew said.

"Drop it boy, good boy, drop it for Stew."
Trumper released the rodent with the shocked look on its
face, its long pink tail hanging loose.

"I bet you can eat 'em though. They are still
meat."

"Stew, why not just leave it, hey, not do all the
cutting apart and showing me the liver and lungs again. I
don't sleep right after one of your autopsies."

"It's how you learn, its how da Vinci learned."
he said.

"He learned to paint by cutting open rats and
pigeons?"

"Yeah," he picked up the flaccid creature by that
pink tail. "Learned how the muscles all worked and made
him a better painter."

"Moaning Lisa will never look the same again." I
declared. I took a run up and leapt across the water onto
the hillside my wet shoes made me slip slowly back into
the water. "For the love of Mike!"

Stew leapt like Nijinsky ... rat in hand and
ambled up the steep slope effortlessly. "Come on
useless." he called as I pulled myself free of the water
with the aid of branches of a tree that grew out of the
hillside.

Trumper simply fell into the water and hopped
out then with further bounds made his way up behind
Stew. I watched on enviously then slid back again,
landing on my face, my nails scratching at the clay.
Crawling seemed my best bet, so on all fours I slowly
made my way upwards.

"Don't feed Trumper any rat, Stew."

"I won't. Hey, Hammy ... the balls gone."

"Do rats even have...? Oh ... you mean my football, don't you?"

I looked tentatively, desperate not to lose my footing again. There was Stew, stood on the top of the hill, blue sky and sunshine coming over the shoulder of his silhouette. Then I saw he had the blinking ball in his hands.

"Catch!"

"What?"

He launched the ball at me. I made an insipid attempt to stop it passing me, lost my grip and fell, roly poly style down again ending with a splash.

He called down.

"Hey, let's play King of the Castle, you try and get up here and I'll try pushing you back down. That'll be funny, won't it, Hammy? Hammy? Where are you?"

I was already taking the long way round, no more climbing, no more falling, no more water in my shoes, no more wet 'grundy's,' no more tee shirt hanging down like I'd pinched it from my dad.

I was going to take the path, get to the grass and lay down in the sun, I was going to let the clothes dry in the baking heat and let wisps of water evaporate in steam form up into the cloudless sky and more importantly, I was going to ignore my lunatic friend for a little while.

Then, when I was dry, and only then, that's when I would do something else, because that's when I was going to turn over onto my back and dry my front ... I had a busy hour ahead.

REMEMBER, REMEMBER, THE 31ST OF SEPTEMBER!

The occupant of the house on Hugo Street raced to open the front door, whoever was banging the knocker was obviously in severe danger, at worst it was a life or death situation. The door was flung inwards and the woman looked out with fear and stress etched across her middle aged face.

Three boys, one pram with a large bundle that appeared tied together roughly in the shape of a human being.

"Penny for the Guy, missus."

"Excuse me?" she asked pulling her eyes from the pram to the face of a street urchin.

"Penny for the Guy... "Stewart said again, then presented the 'Guy' with a sweeping arm towards the bundle.

"Guy Fawkes?" she asked with bemusement.

"Yeah, Guy Fawkes, bonfire night, you know?"

"It's September!"

"What is?" he asked.

"It's only September, bonfire night is in November!" she said harshly.

"Are you sure?" he asked her then turned to me with a questioning face.

"I think bonfire night might have been moved this year, miss, because it keeps raining and the fires go out, so they've moved it, yeah, that's what I think." I said rather more convincingly than I expected.

"Moved bonfire night? It has to be November the 5th, that's when it took place, you can't have bonfire night on another night." she said as she folded her arms slowly and a wall of scepticism was suddenly confronting us.

"Course they can!" Stew said insistently.

"Yeah, that's right, two years ago it was on the 4th of November." I agreed.

"That was one night, and only because it would of fell on a Sunday. They are not going to move it two months."

"What, are you like a 'polistician'?"

"A what?"

"A polistician, a member of 'Pearlyment'?" Stew carried on.

"I just know they wouldn't change the date of bonfire night by that much, little boy!"

"Well no wonder Guy Fawkes wanted to blow the 'Pearlyment' up if the other 'polisticians' are all like you. Awkward, and not believing normal people like me and Hammy. We might just not burn our Guy, we might burn an 'iffigee' of you."

"Yeah, bet Guy Fawkes had trouble with people like you, bet he was just a happy man until you lot made him so mad he wanted to blow you all up." I edged closer to my friend as I gave him my support.

"I am not a politician or a Member of Parliament, I am just saying it's highly unlikely they would change the date." she looked slightly upset at the thought of a lookalike rag doll being incinerated by these too children.

"Ha, highly unlikely ... but not impossible, so, a penny for the Guy, Miss ... please" Stew jammed his hand out inches from the cold, crossed arms of the bemused lady.

"Who is it, Dorothy?" a voice called from inside her house.

"Two boys, Guying!"

"Guying? What do you mean?"

"They say bonfire nights been moved back two months." she started to smile now.

"They're pulling your leg, Doe, let me sort this." his words getting were louder as he approached the door.

The man was large with a big balding head, his torso was wide and heavy beneath a checked shirt, the hand he placed on the ladies shoulder to move her aside was the size of a coal shovel. I gulped and edged back towards the pram, Stews outstretched hand shook ever so slightly ... but stayed in position.

"Let me see these two shucksters." he said as he first looked at Stew and then when he failed to make him break his stare he turned to me. Luckily I was checking my laces on my slip on shoes at that moment and missed the chance of an eyeballing competition.

"So, bonfire night. When has it been moved to then?"

"The 31st." Stew said confidently.

"Of September?"

"Yep!"

"31st of September." his face grinning and his right hand rubbing his bristly Desperate Dan chin.

"Yep!" he replied with more certainty.

"Here's me thinking there are only 30 days in September!" his eyebrows raised ever so slightly as his eyes widened.

"What?"

"Last time I looked there were only 30 days in September. Has that changed too?"

"Er, 30 days have October, Avril, June and Cucumber ... all the rest have 31, except ... erm, that month with 28... "

"February?" the man helped.

"Yeah, February which can have other days added or taken away depending on the weather! There, see!"

"See what?" he asked "Half of that was gobbledygook! For a start, which month is Cucumber?"

"I think he mean to say that what they've done is take one day out of Cucumb... I mean November and borrowed it to September just for this year. They are just testing to see if it works better." I tried desperately to undig this very deep hole.

"Oh, Jeff, just give 'em a 'threpny' bit, Corra's on in a minute. We can't stand here listening to these two raving nutcases all night."

"Let me see this Guy first, I'm not giving these drips any money for a rubbish Guy Fawkes." the giant of a man said to her face then turned and bent down with his large backside on his heels. "Mmmm, shabby coat, legs are a bit short... "he squeezed the leg feeling the newspaper that had been balled and shoved in, bits of dried, corn coloured, grass stuck out of the arms and legs by the gloves and shoes.

"Don't think it's worth anything more than the penny they are asking Doe, look at this mask..." he pulled it upwards and revealed the horror filled face of David Marsden, open mouthed and wide eyed.

"What the ....?" the man squealed and jumped back like he had looked Satan in the face. "Is he alive?"

"Yeah, we're taking him for a walk." I said.

"Oh, the poor thing." the woman stepped over her husband, who sat on his backside still in shock. "Are you okay, son?" she asked the four year old boy.

"Yes." he said meekly.

"Have these horrible boys made you dress like this?"

"No, we are playing bonfires. I'm a dummy and got to be quiet."

"Does your mother know you've been dressed like this?" she asked.

"If we can have our 'threpence', miss, we'll just bugger off." Stew offered stepping between child and woman.

"I don't think this is legal, you can't truss up little boys and pass them off as Guy's. Take him home, immediately." she insisted.

"So one minute she's a 'polistician', now she's a 'bannister'! You're a right jack of all 'trains', aren't cha?" he mumbled under his breath.

232

"Listen, I'll give you a shilling. But only if you take him home and get all this rubbish out of his clothes. Deal?"

"Deal!" I said instantly.

"Wait, we have only just started, we might make a bomb outside the Lightbowne pub."

"I want to play bonfire men..." Dave cheered.

"Jeffrey, get up off your fat backside and go get my purse out of the living room, come on you big lummox." he raised himself to his feet and grimaced with evil intent at both Stew and me.

"Go and get her purse, Jeffery... bobbles bon bon!" Stew said smiling around at me referring to the new series on ITV, The Lovers."

"Hey, you cheeky little bleeder!" the man made a move towards the three of us.

"Just go and get the purse, go on." she had held her thin arm to stop his move.

He turned and was away for less than thirty seconds before he passed her an old, well-worn brown leather purse. He then growled at Stew who was stood with a grin that would have looked at home on a happy cat from Cheshire.

"Here, a shilling between you two and you," she leaned down to Dave, "and you, you can have a shilling of your own, you deserve it."

"Oh fink you, missus." his tiny alabaster hand now free of the grey mitten grasped the coin.

"I think you've got off cheaply, we could have demanded more. That's our night over... "

"Get on with you, make sure he gets home safe. We have a deal, okay." she said insistently.

"Deal!" Stew said reluctantly, then spat in his right palm. It was a large mouthful of spittle, not without a little heavy phlegm in there. The wet hand was offered up to a shocked lady.

"Do you know? I'm going to take your word on this occasion, no need for a handshake." she raised her hands up to her chest like she was surrendering.

"We don't lie, miss." I said.

"No, course you don't! Bonfire night in September...!? Go on, bugger off."

The money was pocketed by Stew and I began pushing the pram with our 'Guy' in it towards the shops on Lightbowne road.

"Dave, we are going to teach you all about sharing now."

"I like learning fings."

"Yeah, that's good. I'm sure we have enough money for a bubbly gum for you!" Stew smiled at me, conspiracy afoot.

"Yay, I love bubbly's!" he squealed.

"Yay," Stew echoed, "Now let me look after your money, and pull your mask back down, just in case we see somebody. We might make a few more bob for bommie night."

"But we promised!" I said.

Stew held up a saliva ridden hand before my eyes.

"We never shook ... it's not a deal if you don't shake." he smiled as he wiped the 'goz' on his shorts.

SHRINKING VIOLET

"Are you sure, missus?" Stew looked dumbfounded by her words.

"I'm absolutely certain..." she smiled. "...the next stop is Wilmslow and then Crewe and after that London Euston." her final smile was one of consolation, then she returned to her book.

"Flamin' 'eck, Hammy, we're on the wrong train!" Stew said.

"Are you definite that Poynton isn't the next stop?" I was interrupted by a bing bong, the lady looked towards the tannoy rather than me.

"Next Station stop ... Wilmslow ... please remember to take all items with you, next stop, Wilmslow."

"Bugger!" I said, the lady mouthed the word 'sorry!'

"What we gonna do?" Stew asked.

"We'll have to get off, then go back to Stockport, get the train for Poynton from there." we were supposedly off to Poynton Pools, a swimming day out, an adventure for two so young.

"Should we just see if there's a swimming pool here, at Wilmslow?" he suggested in a deflated tone.

"Erm...well, I suppose we could ask near the station, as long as we don't waste the whole day." the

236

train squealed and squeaked to a halt, this was the days of slam door coaching stock, I grabbed the brass handle and pushed it down, heaved the heavy door outwards and stepped out into the warm, sultry morning, Stew followed and before we could walk away the platform guy shouted for us to close the coach door, Stew turned and kicked it with heel of his Wayfarers, there was a satisfying clunk as it locked itself in place.

The train conductor looked up and down the length of the train. The man who worked the platform whistled confirming all door locked he leapt aboard, pulled his door to, and hung himself out of the sliding window, there was a whistle and the pair exchanged green flag waves … the train took power and slowly rolled away from the platform. Stew turned to me and suggested driving trains would be the best job in the world, I doubted it, how could it possibly compete with being a helicopter pilot.

We wandered down the sloping path that lead out of the train station, we exited onto a roundabout and the only obvious route was a right turn down a road past a garage with large collection of expensive cars on the forecourt. Stew insisted on drifting onto the forecourt and peering into the Jaguar and Bentley's on sale. There was lots of leather and walnut veneer on show and for two boys from Moston, the opulence was an entire Universe away, neither of our parents owned a car, but both our dads had vehicles they brought home from work. Stew's dad had a large white van with a box on the back, and my dad parked his forty foot Seddon Atkinson, articulated lorry by the side of our house.

"Can I help you?" a man's voice called from behind us.

"Yes, is there a swimming pool here?" I asked.

"Here? On a premier sales forecourt?" he shook his head at such a bizarre question.

"Noooo. Not in here with the cars … here in Wilmslow?" Stew swung the plastic bag he was holding wide, hitting a Rolls Royce as he tried to indicate he meant anywhere close by.

"Oh no, no, no watch the cars. I'm not sure about any swimming pool, now can you not walk near the cars please, they are very, very expensive."

"We're only taking a ganders, mister."

"I beg to differ, careful with that bag! And look at the finger prints here!" he rubbed with his jacket at the smudge.

"I think that might be my nose, actually, sorry." I apologised.

The man stopped suddenly and checked his jacket for bogies.

"Can you just vacate the premises, please?" he opened his arms and guided us like sheep onto the pavement.

Stew turned to me, and suggested they spoke a different language in Cheshire. We made our way off the lot, plastic bags, swimming attire inside, swinging gaily by our side.

The heat was becoming intense as the day closed in on midday, the sun was high in the cloudless, Cheshire sky and my forehead soon had droplets forming, and ready to fall.

"We need to see someone, we can't just walk and walk." I said.

"There's some shops coming up on the right." he pointed to a row of Olde Worlde frontages, all black and white in an Elizabethan style. We walked on hoping to see someone.

"We can ask in the shops if there's no-one about." Stew suggested.

The first window was an estate agents, some of the houses on display were on offer for over £70,000!! We were aghast, that was not just a pools win, it was a large pools win! The man inside the shop, shooed us away with a nonchalant wave of disgust. Stew pressed his nose on the plate glass and stuck out his tongue, much to the chagrin of the dark suited chap inside.

Next along was a second hand shop with valuable looking artefacts, an atlas globe, with the top hemisphere snapped open revealing a drinks shelf inside and cut glass beakers set in the wooden interior. But the things that really took our eye was the three stuffed animals, a large stags head … Stew explained how you probably used this near the front door to hang your coats on its antlers. There was an owl with very wide, large eyes. Stew suggested with a grin that it had eyes like this because the man who had stuffed it had shoved his hand up its bum to put the filling inside. Last but not least was the head of a lion, mid-roar, attached to the wall just by the window. Stew was in total awe of its size, and announced that on getting his first job he was getting the train back down here to buy it for over his bed.

After perusing the windows of the first two shops we moved on. A walls ice cream sign hanging above the next shop doorway hinted at sweets, and more importantly, drink. The heat had become dehydrating and a cold orange drink would be perfect. First Stew delved into his pocket and pulled out a sixpence.

"I've got a tanner." he declared.

"I have sevenpunce. Two 'threpneebits' and a penny." I held my hand out with the three coins sat in my palm.

"Come on, let's see what they've got." Stew said.

We walked into the shop, our plastic bags bumping on our knees, then looked in the upright, open fridge but it held milk, butter and cold meats.

"You got any Jubbly's, mister?" I called to the balding man in the white overcoat, arms crossed, but smiling.

"In the freezer to your right, son." he pointed at a box freezer with sliding glass doors on the top.

"How much are they?" Stew quizzed.

"Tuppence … orange or blackcurrant, nice and frozen, just about perfect for this heat, hey boys?"

"Yeah, I'm absolutely melting, mister." I wiped my brow to emphasise my words.

Stew delved into the box freezer after he had slid the glass top across. I swear he nearly tipped himself in, his feet had left the floor and kicked out wildly as he searched amongst the frozen wares inside, then suddenly, like a pearl diver resurfacing for air he reappeared, holding orange and a purple triangular packages, one in each hand...and the smile of a successful gold prospector.

240

"Do you want orange, Hammy?" he asked.

"Yeah, that's fine." I placed a coin on the glass counter while Stew brought them from the rear of the shop. "I'll want a penny change, mister, please." I was just making sure he realised.

"Aren't you the mathematician, young lad?" he smirked. "Now, do you want me to open them?" he held up a pair of small, stainless steel scissors, then chopped them open and shut, a full toothed smile on his face.

"Oh yeah, brilliant, thanks mister." both were laid on the counter and each had the top trimmed to allow access to the icy refreshment. He passed them down, purposefully giving me the blackcurrant and Stew the orange just to tease.

"A brand new penny for you ... and are you paying, or are you robbing my store, son?" he smiled at Stew as we exchanged jubblys.

Stewart laid his silver coin on the counter and received four pence change. We headed for the exit sucking and slurping, taking all the colour from the ice.

"Thank you," I cried over my shoulder, then remembered, "...hey mister!" I called from the door.

"Uh uh?" the man turned, scissors and bits of paper in his hand.

"Is there a swimming baths near here?"

"Not that's open, sorry lads."

"Flaming Nora!" Stew exclaimed.

"What are we gonna do?" we stood in the doorway sucking and thinking.

"Excuse me." a small, older woman said as she tried to pass us.

241

"Oh sorry, missus. Flipping 'eck … I think you know my mum, don't you?" I said, startled I knew this lady, so far from home.

"Do I?" the white haired lady said and chortled with an imperceptible shake of her head.

"...or is it my nana you know?" I rubbed my chin trying to gain access to my memory banks.

"Where does your Grandmother live?"

"Ancoats." I declared.

"Now, I was actually born in Ancoats." she said, a smile appeared on her face.

"So was I!!" I volunteered.

"I wasn't!" said Stew, trying to get in on the act.

"Do you go to bingo?" I was trying to put her face into my nana's life.

"No, son. I haven't played bingo in a very long time."

"Oh, you should, my mum won £25 three weeks ago!" I turned to Stew and nodded at him, he was impressed, but apparently not as much as the lady was.

"I think I should start going again if they're giving that sort of cash away! Where does your gran live, in Ancoats?"

"Harding Street, number one, that's where I was born."

"I was born on German Street, its called Radium Street now, they had to change it after the First World War started."

"Cos we were fighting the Germans?" I asked.

"I suspect it was, you can't be living on a street named after the enemy, can you."

"No, I'd hate to live on a street called City street, wouldn't you, Stew?"

"Yeah, I hate City ... but to be honest, I don't mind the Germans." he said honestly

"What are you doing boys?" she glanced down at our dress, both in Bri-nylon tee shirts, my orange collar had one side up and the other laid flat. Stews cream one looked like he'd borrowed it off his dad, it hung off him. Both our knees were dark, not muddy, but a colour that suggested a firm brush would be required to get out the ingrained dirt. And neither of our long socks were above our ankles...they were bundled and crumpled just above our scuffed, black shoes.

"We were going Poynton Pools, but Stew made us get the wrong train!" I thumbed my hand at my pal.

"I didn't make you get on it, did I? We both got the wrong train ... I didn't have to give you a Chinese burn or anything, did I?"

"...then we got off here," I ignored his claims of innocence. "...and there isn't a swimming pool near here, so we are just thinking what to do, while we suck on our Jubbly's." I explained while Stew stared daggers at me.

"Oh dear, so you're both hot and bothered, then?"

"We are, we might get some chips and then get the train back to Manchester, and it'll take too long to get to Poynton Pool now."

"Well, boys, I'm just getting some mints, then how do you fancy joining me for a cream tea?" she indicated towards a shop a couple of doors down, that had chairs and tables on the pavement.

243

"Urghh...cream in tea that sounds horrible." Stew said to the ground.

"No, son, cream cakes and a nice refreshing pot of tea ... or cola if you fancy that." she explained to us.

"My mum said I can't take anything off strangers." Stew said.

"She's not a stranger, she my nana's friend, aren't you?" I piped up, cream cakes on my mind.

"Apparently so!" she smiled again. "Just give me a minute and we can have a lovely lunch, sandwiches, cold drinks and a selection of cakes...mmm...now doesn't that sound nice?"

"Alright, 'spose it can't hurt, cakes and coke!" Stew decided she posed little or no actual threat to our lives.

While she was in the shop Stew interrogated me on who she was. I explained that I knew her face, and she was from Ancoats ... so what was the problem? He just thought it was weird, she didn't dress like someone from Ancoats and he was certain Ancoats folks didn't do cream tea's.

"Okay boys." she was looking down at her hands as she closed her purse then put it and her newly purchased mints in her leather shopping bag. She then looked up and smiled "...let's go and eat." We walked behind her, her heels clacking on the pavement, our ice's being sucked dry for the few doors we travelled to the cafe. When she pushed open the door a cold burst of air hit us, it was even more refreshing than the fast disappearing Jubbly's ... and they were really gorgeous!

"Hello, Terence, can we have a table for three please?" she spoke gently to a brylcreemed man with a claret waistcoat on, who smiled and bowed slightly.

"Of course, Mrs. Carson." the name not helping us with her identity.

He lead us to a small round table, a pristine, snow white, linen tablecloth covered its surface. The lady sat after the waiter pulled her chair out for her with a squeal from the legs. Me and Stew just squeezed in and up onto the chairs, smiling at each other, completely amazed at the nice lady's generosity. Stew laid his Jubbly down while he tried to edge his chair nearer to the table, both hands on the seat, swinging his legs and torso, little by little and with excruciating scraping noises he finally had his chest pressed against the table's edge. While he concentrated on this he failed to notice juice spreading like purple blood from his Jubbly that was resting on the table cloth.

"Arhhhh!!! It's not my fault!" Stew exclaimed, picking up his purple Jubbly, "Its cos they make the packet triangular … you can't stand 'em up!" he held it up to prove how difficult it was rest one without losing even more melted fluids.

"I'm sorry, Terence. I'm sure you understand, don't you?" she spoke softly to the man whose face had begun to tense up. His jaw was clamping his perfect teeth together, but her words suddenly relaxed him, he smiled at her and nodded gently.

"It isn't a problem, madam, honestly, it could easily happen to anybody." he smiled again.

"Oh, jolly good. Could you bring us a large pot of tea and three cream scones and a small selection of your lovely cakes please? The boys are famished, aren't you? Oh, and two Coca Cola's with ice, please."

We both nodded in tandem. Stew both arms on the table and me holding my hands on my lap. Scones sounded lovely, although she pronounced it wrong!

He disappeared, writing on a small notepad while he walked. Before we could start talking a little girl from another table approached our new friend.

"Can I have your autograph please, Mrs. Carson?" she smiled sweetly and twisted her little body as she spoke.

"Of course you can..." me and Stew exchanged befuddled glances. "...I have these photographs from the studio." she took the pen from the girl and began writing across the picture. "What's your name dear?" she waited for her reply and then finished.

As the girl thanked her and then returned to her smiling parents on their table I was able to see the picture, and who the picture was of.

"Are you off Coronation Street?" confusion on my face.

"I am, my dear." she whispered secretly as she leaned over towards me. "But keep it under your hat" I felt my hair, I had no headwear! "I mean, let's keep it a secret, please." she nodded as she spoke.

"You're Ena Sharples! But without the fishing net on your hair!" Stew said, a little too loudly.

"Yes, but let's keep it to ourselves, hey?" she spoke a little firmer now.

"D'you know Hilda Ogden and Annie Walker then?" I asked in a hushed tone.

"Well, yes, I suppose I do."

"Are they alright? Nice, like?"

"They are lovely. As are all the cast, we are like a big family, really ... all good friends."

"What's your name again? In real life?" I asked.

"Violet ...Violet Carson."

"That's it! My dad calls you Violent Carson! He says you're a right miserable bugger." I swung round in my seat to stare at this outburst from my friend. Mrs. Carson just smiled. "...I'm just saying what he said. I never said it, I don't watch it! But my dad says you are always angry, even with your little mate Minnie 'Coldwell.'"

"Yeah, but you don't have to say it to her face ... she's nice in real life. She's buying us Coke, cakes and ...'skownes'..." I looked towards her...she nodded. I pronounced it just like her.

"I know! She's just acting like a witch."

"Boy's, boy's, its fine. That's is just what my character is like ... grouchy and opinionated, and if your father thinks that, then I'm doing a good job."

"Oh good, 'cos we are not rude, or anything, we know how to behave." There was a large slurp as I sucked the last remnants of orange from the little bit of ice that remained in my carton ... the little that was left was anaemic, white ice, no flavour. I popped this into my mouth and crunched it, facing 'Ena', smiling all the way through the process ... my mouth agape.

"Was that nice?"

247

"It was lovely, missus ... I can't believe we are with someone famous."

Suddenly Terence appeared, tray in hand, supporting a large white teapot and three cups. He laid them before us while we watched in silence, apart from whispered thank you's.

Me and Stew refused the offer of tea and said we'd wait for our cold drinks. Tea didn't make sense to us, we were hot enough without pouring steaming hot drinks down our throats.

Terence returned with cakes and glasses of Coca Cola, chinking with ice. We both immediately supped at the Coke, and moments later released a very large, synchronised...'arghhhhhh.'

Ena, offered us chocolate topped pastries with thick yellowish cream stacked inside them. Stew went for the éclair, he ignored the fork and pushed half of it into the chasm that was his mouth. He chomped down and the cream oozed from the choux pastry that remained in his hand. His top lip now had a chocolate moustache and there was cream in each corner of his mouth. While he chewed he brought up his right forearm and wiped it across the surface of his mouth ... his eyes were wide and happy.

I followed suit, no fork and wide mouth. My fairy cake was devoured in two, I consciously counted my fingers after I eaten it, just made sure I hadn't chewed one off in the eating frenzy!

"Well, I like to see boys with a good appetite...and you two have fantastic appetites...!" she laughed out loud.

248

"These...(chomp)...are...(wipe mouth)...the best cakes...(lick all around mouth)...I have ever..(suck teeth for any stuck cream) tasted!" I said with complete satisfaction. Stew took a slurp of his Coke and burped in complete agreement.

"Well, boys. There's the scones to come yet, I hope you are still hungry." Ena said as she lifted a forkful of pastry up towards her mouth.

"Oh yeah, I loves cakes, me mum makes 'em on Saturday and Sunday's for all me Aunties. They come over from Ancoats to sit and talk on Sunday, they gab all day." I said.

"Well, family days are nice. Do you have a lot of Aunties come over?" she asked once she'd finished her chewing.

"Flipping 'eck, he's got about twenty." Stew declared.

"No, I haven't, there's Sue, Jen, Marg, Mary and Jean comes sometimes … and me Uncle Gud, he goes to the pub with me dad."

"Not quite twenty, but a lot!?" Ena said laughing.

"Mum bakes cakes and makes trifle and Sunday lunch and butties."

"Do you have a big house?" she said wide eyed at the spread and family size.

"Naw...ha ha...just one room with the telly and then there's the kitchen downstairs and upstairs my bedroom and my mum and dads bedroom."

"...and the bathroom, I suppose?"

"No … that's in the yard." a little embarrassed to admit it.

249

"We've got a bathroom and toilet upstairs..." Stew interjected proudly.

"Big head." I pulled my tongue out at him.

"Well, I'm sure it's lovely, you wouldn't get all the family coming down if wasn't." Ena smiled and patted my hand.

"It is ... but I would like an inside loo to be honest. I hate peeing in a bucket in the middle of the night, my mum goes mad if I miss it, and to be honest I'm not a good shot when I'm knackered."

"Who is?" she burst into a giggle.

"Are you married missus?" I asked.

"I was, but that was a long time ago. He's sadly not here anymore."

"Where is he?" Stew asked through a mouthful of cream and pastry.

"Joseph died...just three years after I married him...he was so lovely."

"Did you not get married again? Stew butted in ... head now on his folded arms resting on the table.

"No ... I only ever loved him ... strange but sometimes I still feel him close...even now, sixty years later." she looked up at the ceiling wistfully.

"Sixty years ... flamin' Nora!" Stew said.

"I know ... but it only feels like it was yesterday."

"Sixty years." he said again.

"Yes. A full sixty years."

"Sixty ye..."

"Stew, we know how long ago it was." I jumped in quickly.

"I know … but sixty years."

"Yes, and I'm still missing him and thinking about him every day."

"Did you have any kids?" Terence placed the scones down over our shoulders, making me jump initially I thought someone was trying to nick my swimming kit in the plastic bag next to me.

"Thank you, Terence." he smiled and took away the empty plates and Ena's half eaten éclair. "...no...no children and so no grandchildren either, and I love kids too."

"Awww, what a shame, me nana had ten kids! Now she's got a load of grandkids too." I said.

"I think she must have had mine!" she laughed but it was tainted with melancholy.

"Well … What if I be your pretend grandkid? I can call you nana, if you want?" I said, sitting up tall in my chair.

"Yeah, me too. You can never have too many nana's, especially at birthdays and Christmas!!" Stew chortled.

"How nice of you. What lovely children … I bet your parents are very proud of you." she patted my hand.

"Errr, not a lot." Stew admitted, looking down under the table at his scuffed shoes.

"Mine are..." I said vaingloriously.

"Now who's the big head?" Stew whispered to me.

"Well, I'm sorry but they are … you could behave a bit better and maybe they'd be happier, it's not rocket science, Herr Hitler!!"

251

"I do try. It's just the things they don't like me doing ... well ... they're the things I really love to do! It's a shame they can't be proud of what I'm good at." he kicked the leg of the table as he spoke.

"What, like nicking football cards from Dave's shop?" I then changed my voice to a bad impression of Stew's mum. "I am so proud of my little Stewart, he's nicked loads of stuff from the shop. He's dead smart. He ... ouch! Hey, did you just kick me?"

"No, it was Ena Sharples.!" he spat back at me.

"Boy's, please stop arguing. I am sure you will grow up to do something your mother and father can be proud of Stewart." she nodded to confirm his name, he nodded back, grimace to a mini smile in seconds.

"Yes, he's a cat burglar, you know? I'm so pr...ouch. Will you stop kicking me, please?!"

"It was Ena again, wasn't it?" he asked her with a Cheshire cat smile.

"No, Stewart, it wasn't. Brian, stop teasing, Stewart, stop kicking. Let's be civilised, please." she asked firmly.

We both shook hands to bury the hatchet and turned our thoughts to the scones. Like bricklayers, we laid the cream first, it was a thick mortar of yellow. Then we lashed a heavy layer of jam on top of that before putting the lid of the scone on top ... they both ended up looking like confectionary versions of the leaning tower of Pisa!

Carefully lifting them to our mouths, we stopped and contemplated our creations ... mainly just trying to work out a way of getting them into mouths.

We nibbled at them gently, then licked between the scones at the cream, slowly reducing their mass. Not squeezing too hard, but just enough to press out the excess cream into the gaps we had previously cleared with our insistent tongues. Cream scone eating had now become a spectator sport ... Ena gazed on with her fork halfway to her mouth, Terence stood back with a ready towel ... and the other family two tables away just stared on with open mouths.

But nothing deterred us, we managed to excavate the scones filling and begin biting at the actual baked part of our treat. We never bothered to rest, we had a job to do defeat was not an option. Eventually we looked up from our cream splattered hands and smiled a dairy smile. Jam was attached to our top lips and cream was on the tips of our noses and in our nostrils. After pointing at each other's faces and falling about laughing we licked and sucked on each digit and finally wiped our mouths on the back of our hands rather than on the serviettes provided ... Moston style.

"Brilliant that, wasn't it, Stew?" I looked like an extra from a Charlie Chaplin movie. One that had ended with a cream pie fight!

"Yeah, brill. We can't go swimming now though, not on a full belly."

"You won't be able to swim for a month, I think you're liable sink like stones!" Violet said with a shake of her head.

"Ahhh, we'll be fine in a bit, we just need to walk it off." I said confidently.

"You're not thinking of walking home are you? She asked.

"No way..." said Stew. "...we need to go back to the station and get the train back to Manchester.

"I don't really think you should be out this far from home at your age." she said into the large bag she had popped onto her knee. Her head came up and she had her purse in her hand.

"Whatcha doing?" I queried.

"I think it would be better if you got a taxi back home." she said kindly, then indicated to Terence she needed him.

"Yes, Miss Carson?" he asked as he walked towards our table.

"Could you order a black taxi cab for … for my two grandchildren please?" she looked away from the waiter and smiled at both of her new 'grandchildren.'

He looked at the two urchins with food matter attached to all parts of their faces and when they smiled at him, disclosing unchewed food in and about their teeth, he took a step back, aghast.

"Certainly. I'll order it straight away!" he turned and headed towards his desk in the corner.

"Thank you Terence. Do you two want to go and use the lavatory before it gets here? Tidy yourselves up?"

"Yeah, why not? But what's a lavatory?" Stew asked.

"It's a loo, dear." she pointed to a door at the back of the cafe, there was a white stick man painted on it.

We nodded climbed down from our chairs and headed towards the door.

"That was brill, wasn't it?" Stew said.

"It was the best food I've ever tasted … eeeerppppp!!!" The burp had started low in my belly and lasted a little too long and sounded way too loud for a child to produce. I turned round to see the family staring at me from their table.

"…excuse me!!" I apologised with an embarrassed wave of my hand and reddening cheeks.

"She's alright, isn't she?"

"She's more than just alright...she's lovely." I said, holding the toilet door wide for Stew to walk in.

"Hey, I've never been in a taxi before, it'll be like being famous." I looked in the sparkling mirror to see a face in need of a good wash. During my wash I managed to splash Stew and drop the soap onto the tiled floor. The wash was cursory, I was careful not to wash any further south than my chin or go anywhere near my ears, why change the habit of a lifetime now? Stew washed himself, pulling a horrible face as the water hit his mush, he hated water even more than I did! Once we decided we were both passably clean it was time to pull on the rotating towel dispenser, maybe twenty times more than really necessary! With dried hands and faces and red jam stained towelling hanging down, it was time to return to our famous friend. On the cloth. Stew suggested she'd probably done a runner and we'd be put into slave labour in the kitchens and have to wash pots for the next six months.

We tentatively popped our heads round the door and there she sat, dealing Terence five pound notes. She took the receipt and folded a note into the hand of a very happy waiter who bowed twice in thanks at her generosity. She looked up and smiled, I noticed the large, low hung dark bags of her eyes. They made her look very tired but she was very happy to see us all cleaned up. She was so unlike that television character she played so convincingly. Not as harsh and never a hint of Ena's chiselled, downward frown. It was the smile that softened her and allowed us to see she was the owner of an enormous and generous heart. Here we were, two waifs adrift in Wilmslow, and this refined lady finds time to feed and adopt us ... what a wonderful person she truly was.

The taxi came soon after, we climbed dutifully into the back and fastened our seat belts. The diesel engine throbbed and rumbled while Stew explained to the driver exactly where we lived ...mumbled a price for the journey to our host and Miss Carson handed the man a note. She finally put her head through our window.

"Take care, boys, I hope you enjoyed yourselves."

"It was brilliant, Mrs. Sharples ... absolutely brilliant." Stew said gleefully.

"Thanks, missus ... it was great." I agreed.

"Goodbye, Brian and Stew." she waved and stood back from the taxi.

"Goodbye, nana." she grinned widely and stepped back as the driver gunned a reluctant engine. We waved frantically through the rear window as the taxi accelerated slowly away. We carried on waving as she became smaller and smaller, shrinking away ... our very own shrinking Violet.

It's funny how when you really want someone to see you ... you know, like when you're in a taxi, or when you keep a ball up for a hundred, there just never anyone around to witness your success. And so it was for us ... the taxi dropped us at the top of our deserted street, we hopped out ready to impress our peers. Moston was deserted ... not even Nelly Owen was about to shout abuse at us.

"Oh bugger..." Stew said looking at his empty hands.

"What? It's alright she's already paid!"

"No. I've only gone and left me trunks in the bog at the cafe." he kicked the tyre of the taxi in frustration.

"Oh no! Me too ... flipping 'eck." I looked for something to kick but decided slamming the taxi door too hard would have to do.

"Me mums gonna murder me...it was one of her good towels."

"It'll be alright when they hear we've had dinner with Ena Sharples though ... hey?" I suggested.

"Maybe, maybe not." he said half-heartedly.

It was the negative version, because no one ever believed our Sharples encounter, we had no proof. No autograph, our mums thought it was just a ludicrous excuse for lost bathing equipment. But each time she appeared in the snug in the Rovers and I would pipe up...

"She's really nice in real life, you know?"

"Course she is Brian, course she is." they would say before laughing at my serious face.

"But...." I would start, but it was pointless, they just thought I was deluded.

When she passed away, they were taken aback at how upset I got at the loss of this harridan of Corra ... this haggard old dear with the hairnet and a face chiseled from Ancoats granite. But they never knew her like me and Stew knew her, and they were not her honorary grandchildren!

The X..mas Factor

"I can't feel my toes, Brian!" the voice was tiny, there was guilt about the complaint.

"Can you get him to stop whining, please, Hammy?" Stew darted at me.

"He said his feet are frozen!" I tried to explain to my older but much less empathetic friend.

"Well he shouldn't be wearing girl's sandals in this weather, should he?" he said as he approached the large white wooden door.

"Maybe not. But I don't think Kath thought we would be traipsing him all round Moston in three inches of snow!" I explained.

"Shush," he disregarded my explanation with a flick of his hand, "right, are you ready. Put Marsy in the front ... they love little blonde kids, it makes the women pull out their purses." he said as he rubbed his cold hands together furiously.

We became a small triangle, Dave the point, me and Stew at his shoulders. Stewart leaned over Dave and banged heavily on the lions head door knocker on St. Georges Drive.

"They're richer down here, some of them have actually bought their houses!"

"What? Like they don't pay rent or nothing? Can you do that?" I asked, surprised that it was possible to actually own a house.

"It's okay now, I can't feel my toes at all. All gone!" Little Dave Marsden smiled angelically up at Stewart and me.

"That sounds like frostbite, doesn't it?" I whispered to Stew, worried about Dave's foot digits.

"He's fine, stop going on. Shush now, they're here." he pointed to the small window above the door where a yellow light had spluttered on.

The door creaked open and a rather large man stood there gazing down with disdain at us. He was wearing a creased, white vest that was bisected by two elasticated black straps that came over his hairy shoulders and attached to his voluminous trousers with metal clips, pulling them up to his man breasts that sat like semi deflated beach balls on his voluminous belly. He took a step back as the three young boys suddenly attacked him with a song.

"We wish you a merry Christmas, we wish you a merry Christmas, WE... wish you a merry Christmas, (deep breath from all) annnnnd a happy New Year!" three hands jettisoned out towards him in a synchronised action. The man stared dismissively. He unfolded his hirsute arms and put his thick hands, deep into his pocket and rattled some copper coins. We stared at the pockets awaiting the retrieval of his meaty mitts and for him to share out his hard earned coin.

We waited several seconds until it became obvious he was not removing them, if anything they were there to protect his money from us.

"Merry Christmas, sir." I said with a smile.

"S'not Christmas for nearly three weeks." the man said then he burped without covering his mouth. I guessed it hadn't been long since he had eaten kippers.

"We're getting out early so we can beat the rush." Stew explained.

"What bloody rush?"

"Well, some of our mates are gonna do this too. You don't want a load of kids banging over and over again, do you? So we are being 'considerating' to you, you see."

"Are you really?" he raised his eyebrows in doubt.

"We are, an'... "Stew looked around at the snow that covered the path down from the gate to the front door. "... 'an we'll shift the snow off your path for two bob!" he grinned.

"Is that included with the song?"

Stewart puffed out his cheeks and his smile said he'd love too but there was some disparate union rule against such a thing.

"Not really, three bob, all in?" Stew suggested.

"How about you just take your merry Christmas and give it a nice walk down my lovely snowy path?" and he started to close the door.

"Hang on!" I said. "Nothing for the song?"

"Three lines? That's not a song, that's a small sentence! Speaking of which, I'd give you all three months for killing that poor Carol!"

"We ain't murdered anyone called Carol! Have we Stew?" Stew thought for a second and shook his head.

"The Christmas Carol, idiot! You murdered the song!" he looked at me with disdain. "Now if you had sang Rudolf? He jangled his money in his pocket and grinned. "I love that song, real Christmassy!"

"Rudolf? What the red nosed reindeer?" I looked at Stew he shook his head and mumbled he knew three lines of that one too.

"I know that!" a high pitched voice cut the air.

"What?" I asked our little blonde castrato.

"I know that song, my Debra taught it me." Dave said as he rubbed his mittened hands together then told us how Debbie, his sister, had taught him the song.

"What, so you know all of it?" I asked.

"I fink so."

"Right, mister. Rudolf the red nosed reindeer by our little mate, Dave Marsden. Me and Stew on backing vocals and harmonies."

"Oh, this should be good. But hurry up I'm only wearing a vest." he said.

"But look at all that hair on your arms and shoulders and chest. It must be like wearing a fur coat!" I said staring at the masses of hair that covered his body.

"Do you mind? I do have feelings you know?"

"Sorry, but I've never seen anybody that hairy."

"That gorilla at Chester Zoo?" Stew piped in.

"Oh yeah, that was hairy." I laughed as I remembered the school trip. "It stank too!"

"Are you saying I stink?" the man interjected.

"What? Noooo, the gorilla did, it was big, fat and another lady gorilla was picking fleas out of his hair." I looked at the man and started to see the similarity. "Nothing like you, mister, nothing at all." I lied.

"Can we just get on with it? Or I'm shutting the door."

"Yeah, yeah." Stew pulled a mouth organ out of his mouth and blew a shrill note. "Right Dave." he pointed at our six year old accomplice.

Rudolf the red nosed reindeer, (reindeer, I repeated as a harmony)

Had a very shiny nose, (what a corker,)

And if you ever saw it, you may even say it glows, (like a light bulb!)

All of the other reindeers (reindeers, Stew joined in too now)

Used to laugh and call him names, (like Pinocchio)

They never let poor Rudolf, (Rudolf)

Join in any reindeer games, (like Monopoly)

Then one foggy Christmas Eve, Santa came to say, (ho, ho, ho)

Rudolf with your nose so bright, won't you guide my sleigh tonight? (hey?)

Then all the other reindeers, (reindeers)

Shouted out and laughed with glee, (he he he)

Rudolf the red nosed reindeer, (reindeer)

You'll go down in history! (like Napoleon!!!)

We cheered and slapped little Marsy on his back, knocking him into the russet red brickwork of the house and then Stew and me congratulated each other on a song well sung. Then we looked up at the man, his features unchanged.

"Awww, come on, mister. That was brilliant." I flung out my arms in a pleading gesture.

"Yeah, that is the best thing we have ever done." Stew added.

Suddenly he let his grim facade slide from his big round face. A hint of a smile and movement from his hairy forearms as they started to rise out of his pockets.

All three sets of children's eyes watched this slow motion evacuation of his hands. He opened a palm and looked at the coinage. Studied it carefully, we were able to see his mind deciding our worth.

"It was good, 'wan' it?" Dave added in his falsetto voice to no one in particular.

"It was not too shabby son! Hey, and you were by far the best. These two idiots nearly ruined it with their stupid add ons. Napoleon? What was all that about?" he shook his head.

"What, it was great. Sad, happy and funny... all that in one song. Perfickt, if you ask me!" I said to him as his left set of sausage fingers started separating the coins in his right palm.

"Well, I wasn't asking and I certainly wouldn't go as far as saying it was perfection. But, I will undoubtedly hear a lot worse in the next three weeks." he said grudgingly.

"Do you want us to come back again then?"

"No I do not!" he said before the last syllable was even out of Stews mouth.

"You sure?" Stew asking him to think again.

"I am certain, and I'm paying you extra now so I don't see you again until next year. Okay?" he looked momentarily up from his palm and stared at us so he he could confirm we understood.

"Extra?" me and Stew sang in harmony again as we smiled at each other, then nodded in agreement we should not return.

"Here," he lifted the largest coin the Royal Mint was creating in 1969. It was large, it was round and it silver coloured.

"Half Crown?" I whispered softly, barely daring to say it aloud in case he hadn't realised what he was about to pass over.

"Right, now bugger off!" he declared as Dave gratefully took the coin from him, it looked gigantic in his small white hand.

"Yes, mister. You sure you don't want your path clearing?" Stew was refusing to let this man off the line.

"I should get it cleared for all that dosh!" he said looking back down at Dave and the coin he was holding up to his face with both hands like a mirror.

Stew grabbed Dave's shoulders and guided him and the money out of the man's reach. He knew he wouldn't venture into the slush outside his door, not with bare feet. Hairy bare feet at that, the man was a Sasquatch!

"Nah, I don't think so, matey." he said as he gently tried lifting the coin from Dave's hands. David's reluctance to let go of the money meant his arms were stretched upwards as Stewart pulled. "Let go, Dave." Stew said encouragingly. The coin was in a tug of war between them, but there was only ever going to be one winner. "Come on, let go. Well done." he added as height and Stews strength proved too much for him and Dave's arms flopped suddenly down by his side.

"Hey now, make sure he gets his fair share." the man called just before he stepped back and closed his door. The light that had flooded the path began to disappear like an eclipse as the door moaned shut. It was only five-thirty, but there was a blue darkness surrounding us now. The heavy clouds that hid the stars and moon from us now decided to begin littering the air with big, fat white snowflakes. They floated slowly, like

265

small white feathers about us, reluctant to actually reach the floor.

"Snowwwww." Dave said as he tried to catch one on his small pink tongue.

Stew held the coin up to me and winked.

"He's forgot about this already!" he laughed, that guilt gene of his had gone missing in action yet again.

"Well, I've got to admit it, Stew, you were right. They are blinking rich down here."

"Hammy!!! I'm always right! Now don't go telling Gary, Digger or Geoff about this. This is going to be like the Californian Gold Rush for the next three weeks! Our first house and we get this." the half crown lifted to my eyeline.

"No. It'll be our secret. But will Kath let us take Dave out every night if the weather is like this? We need him, they'll love him singing in that little baby voice of his."

"We'll just kidnap him if she doesn't" he said dismissively.

"And what if he loses some toes through frostbite?"

"What?" he stopped and looked at Dave who was jogging around a streetlight, chasing snowflakes illuminated by the golden-orange beam from above.

"Look at his feet!" I pointed at the once russet coloured sandals, now dark brown and sodden.

"Dave!" Stew called. "Do you want Bri to give you a 'donkey' ride home?"

"A donkey ride? Yes please, I like donkey rides." he chirruped.

"Is there anything that kid doesn't bloody like?" Stew asked with a head shake.

"He's alright, he's happy." I smiled at him as he skipped back to us.

"Well he's our cash cow, and we are taking care of him. Christmas 1969 is going to go down in history!"

"Yeah." I agreed easily. "Tis the season to be merry!"

"Tis the bloody season to make money, Hammy, pots of money." he rubbed his cold, pink and purple hands together briskly then blew warm air between his pressed palms.

"You look just like Scrooge when you do that!"

"Do I?" he looked sad for a second. "That's nice, he was a poor, misunderstood guy!"

"Really? Scrooge?" I asked with disappointment. Yet another one of Stew's heroes who didn't fit my criteria of heroic.

"Definitely, he was just a businessman trying to make a living." he then grabbed Dave under the armpits. "Come on Tiny Dave, get on Hammy Cratchit's back. All aboard..." He said as he lifted the lightweight boy onto my back. I heard him whisper something in his ear.

"Go on, say it." he encouraged the blonde boy.

"God bless us, ebony one!" he shouted down my lughole joyously, bouncing with each word.

"Near enough!" Stew laughed and trudged ahead through the snow. His right hand came out of his pocket and he flicked the half crown high into the raw December air.

"God bless me, especially!" he laughed. "God bless me and in fact ... sod everyone else!"

JUST A WALK IN THE PARK

"Come on son, foot up, let's tie your lace."

"Ehmmm, what..?" I stretched like a cat as I attempted to wake from my sleep. I opened my eyes slowly, then started back, "Dad!! What ... where?"

"Hello son, come on. Let's get these tied and go out for a walk."

"Dad..." I stared at him in bewilderment." Dad, you're..you've..oh God, no! Please say I've not died? This isn't heaven is it? I can't go yet....! The boys, dad, I can't leave the boy's ... who's going to look after them?" The panic was now all too real.

"Calm down son. I've just popped back down for a walk and a chat ... you are fine and so are the boys." he tried to calm me with his steady and calm tone.

"So ... I've not passed away in my sleep?" I looked down at my legs and arms. "What the...?" these were just the limbs of a child, I had gone back forty years body wise.

"It's fine, calm down and enjoy it!" he stood after he'd finished my laces. "There..." he said with a smile, he was strong again ... a dark, full head of hair, his chest and shoulders were substantial again and there was his familiar engaging smile.

I stood, I was barely up to his dark belt on his jeans. If this was a dream, I decided I was going to run with it … it felt wonderful. I walked into him, I gripped him … hard, squeezed like Mick McManus trying to bring Giant Haystacks down, and then his meaty hand lost itself in my hair as he stroked my head tenderly. Tears came freely and although there was no noise, my chest heaved in sobs. Then he laid both hands on my tiny shoulders, pushing me back, ever so slightly.

"You okay?"

"What's going on dad … am I dreaming?"

"Who knows…?" he smiled again. "...but should we take advantage of this opportunity anyway?"

"Heck yes!" I fell into him again, the embrace even tighter. "I've missed you dad, we all have."

"I'm here now, so let's get out of here." I then took in my surroundings, I realised we were stood in the house in Lakin street … the one we had left back in 1971.

"Here..." he held out his hand, my little paw was lost as it was enveloped by his hard but warm fingers. "...come on." he started walking and the living room that we were in started to fade … the white, patterned wallpaper began to dissolve away before becoming a green backdrop … it was alive … they were leaves! Rhododendron bushes had replaced the simple wallpaper on our left and a long white path opened up ahead of us … a path that was becoming a steep hill.

"Where are we, dad?" I knew this place.

"It's Boggart Hole Clough." he explained.

I twisted around, first to my left and then to my right, of course, we were heading up to the lake. We were about to put our backs into a steep climb and as we ascended I looked to my right, immediately off the path there was a sharp drop into a very deep, but narrow gulley ... one of the 'cloughs' that gave the park its name. The many times I had scrambled down the clay lined sides and leapt across the meagre river at the bottom before clambering the opposite side, up to Carters Field ... scratched, caked in mud and breathing heavily as I watched trailing friends finishing their climb ... my hands on hips and undoubtedly laughing.

Dad pulled gently to help my little legs in the climb to the summit. The rhododendron bushes were heavy with flowers, pastel pinks and blues and as big as footballs. These were to our left and filled in the few spaces between the myriad of large, diverse trees. The green canopy overhead moved gently in a warm breeze, allowing a dabbling of warm sunshine to hit us occasionally through the gaps in branches and leaves, birds sang and in the distance a woodpecker intermittently tapped away at high speed, nature's own Morse code. I looked at my free hand, there was a bamboo stick as long as I was tall, and on the end was a green net.

"We going fishing for tiddler's again?" I asked giggling.

"I thought we would have a chat and you could catch some fish." he held up a jam jar, it had a string handle and it swung lightly in his grasp.

"Come on, nearly there." his encouragement helped ... my thighs had started to burn in my effort ... these kids legs took twice as many strides as my father's long rangy legs.

We eventually topped the brow and the small entrance gate to the boating lake came into view. Fifteen yards to go, it was still a climb and I was tempted to ask dad to carry me, but then decided against it ... I would hate of him to think of me as someone who gives up too easily. The island's trees peeked over a freshly painted, green metal fence and I knew one more minute's effort and I would be rewarded with a view that always stirs something inside.

As we climbed the five steps through the kissing gate, the lake finally came into view ... the sun was bouncing off the unusually clear and clean water like a constantly shimmering starburst of light. There were no bike frames or litter, nothing to spoil this idyllic scene. A flotilla of boats glided easily through the water, couples giggling and smiling as they passed by, their oars splashing as they attempted to pull themselves along.

I raced forward to the water and dropped flat down on a white pavement slab. These strips of heavy stone edged the lake all the way around, and again seemed whiter and cleaner than past memories. I hung my head down to the lake and watched carefully, attempting to see through the water so I could spot my prey ... there, in the water darkened by the shade of the slabs rim, swam a shoal of sticklebacks.

"Quick, pass me my net dad, please." I begged urgently.

"Here you go, son"

I took it and in a swift sweep I managed to catch three or four, I pulled it free of the water and watched glistening droplets of water, each like a diamond, fall, as the net released all but the fish. This was the first time I hadn't also caught 3lb of green weeds and sludge in my fishing net.

"Hey, well done son, you've not lost it, have you?" he laughed.

"Nope, here..." I carefully pulled them free of the netting and one by one dropped them into the jam jar as dad held it close, "..ouch.." the last fish had raised its sharp, defensive dorsal fin, and stabbed it into my soft palm.

"Careful Bri." dad said.

"I'm fine. I'm just glad it didn't wake me up." I replied looking up from my prone position, this changed my dad's look from concern to a concurring smile. "Hey dad, where's our Al?" I continued.

"Your brother? Alan is sat on my shoulders at Chester Zoo as we speak, we're in the monkey house ... and he's giggling away like a right nutter, and I've got ice cream dribbling down my neck"

"They won't let you get out with him, dad. They'll think you've stolen him ... he he."

"Hey, what have you been told? Not funny, he's your brother and he cares about you and your mother immensely."

"I know, dad, I was just joking, he's been really good with mum ... you know, since you've been gone." I said quietly, single tears starting to brim my eyelids.

"I know, and so have you ... the funeral, Bri, it was wonderful, everything I could have wished for ... and when you kissed the coffin it meant a lot."

"Ha, well thanks, it wasn't an easy day. That wind when we opened the hearse tailgate ... was that you?"

"Yeah. I laughed when you looked up, I knew you had realised it was me when you smiled up at the sky."

"I just thought it had to be you ... it was so bizarre."

"Well, thanks for the send off, and thanks for looking after your mum ... and you need to know how proud I am that you are bringing those wonderful boys up so well, all alone. I know it can't be easy." and the pride was there in his eyes for me to see, the tears dropped like lead weights down my cheeks.

I turned over and lay on my back, there was little bits of gravel on the ground that made it slightly uncomfortable, but the warmth of the sun on my face balanced it out. I closed my eyes and drank in the sounds and smells ... I wanted to feel everything.

"No, it's not, but it is my duty, dad. I hope they appreciate it, though, it's been a hard five years since the split, they stood by me and I am trying to keep their lives on an even keel"

"I understand, but it will be rewarding, son. Enjoy this period of your life, they will repay your love a hundred times over in the future. Look at me, I should have been around so much more when you were both little." he said sheepishly.

"Dad, you were working all hours, providing the money to pay bills and give us holidays ... and mum was always there."

"I wasn't working all the time. I took your mother for granted, she was like a single parent at times, the Lightbowne took too much of my time, and like I said … I'm sorry."

"Forgiven. You were always there for me when I needed you, and if you were such a rubbish dad, why do I love you so much? Why do I miss you on a daily basis? Why do I feel this pride in my chest when anybody mentions your name?" I asked, a slight anger creeping into my voice.

"I appreciate that Bri, it means a lot. Family was always the most important thing to me, even if I relied on your mum being the rock that the family was built on. She really was … still is … the most wonderful wife and mum."

"You are pushing against an open door there, dad. She is a bit angry with you though, just slipping away like that."

"I didn't have a say, it was my time … and we all have a time, and my time was in that December evening."

I opened my eyes again to see Kenyon Lane coming into view. The Ben Brierley, all white and black, on our right, the Museum was behind crossed Moston Lane and down past the Co-op on our left.

"We finished in the park?"

"Yep, time to walk home, son … with our prize, though!" he held up my three fishes.

"It was a real shock when you … you know? It left us in a real state."

"All done now ... you can't worry about the past, worry about the things you can affect, like the thief that surrounds us all."

"Thief?" I looked around.

"Yes, and he steals from under your nose, hiding in plain sight."

"Who, dad...?" I was at a loss to what he was talking about.

"Time, son ... there are clocks, watches and phones all showing us the time ... and as each minute drops off there are too many sitting on their backsides procrastinating or watching telly, and then, when the grey hair takes over and the limbs start to fail they will regret missed opportunities ... and then they will cry about all the wasted years. Don't be one of those son, do the things that make you happy, and do them often." the passion built in his voice as he spoke. "...it's all over all too soon, Bri...believe me, I know!"

"I see, you're telling me to get off my fat backside, aren't you?"

"No ... I'm telling you not to regret anything, son."

"...are you telling me to let someone in to my life?" I queried.

"Just start bringing down that wall ... it's been too high for too long, and you weren't made to be alone, not someone like you!" he stared me out, I dropped my eyes to my scuffed size 3 shoes.

"I'm not alone, I have the boys ... I have...."

"They will eventually fly away son, as is right, and alone is such a lonely furrow to hoe." he interrupted.

276

"I'll see ... I'm not just going to grab first girl I see." I smiled at the very thought.

"No, I think that might still be illegal. Just keep your options open and be prepared for a change." he winked.

"Okay ... hey, do you know something I don't?"

"Yes, I do, but rules are rules ... can't tell." he laughed, and tapped the side of his nose.

"Spose the lottery numbers are out of the question, then." I turned and looked up at him, grinning with a full set of young teeth.

"Really, Bri?!" he sounded surprised, we had reached the record shop and its door was open and Life on Mars was escaping on to the Lane, Rick Wakeman was in the middle of his iconic piano solo, I took a second to answer as I let it flow over me.

"Naw, dad. I'm joking. As you always said, I've already won the lottery of life, English ... Mancunian and nearly as good looking as you. That's before taking into consideration the fact I had the best mum and dad in the world, and such good memories of laughter and love in our house"

"Thank goodness I did something right. Money really isn't all it's made out to be ... whereas love is ... and so much more on top of that."

"You're preaching to the choir, dad. Hallelujah!" I laughed out loud and waved jazz hands above my head.

"I hope so ... you certainly can't buy it!" his turn to laugh

"Beatles record dad ... ha ha. Please don't start quoting songs to me, please."

"Hey, they can be a good way of getting a message across, Desperado. So why don't you come to your senses ... let somebody love you ... before it's too late." a large smirk spread across his face. "The Queen of hearts is always your best bet!"

"Really, dad? The Queen of Hearts ... does she even exist? Here, try this one ... Papa ... don't preach!" I stopped and put my hands on my hips ... top that father!

"Touché ... I'll have that one Bri, but there is a rainbow above you" he persisted with the Eagles theme as we walked, passing the Galleon restaurant now.

"Leave it now ... enough with the lyrics. Hey, wait up..." there was now a soft orange sun setting on the horizon and it was dim enough to look straight into, it was just dropping down below the rooftops and dad was getting ahead of me with his long strides.

"Catch up, come on slowcoach."

I began running ... there was no aching in my right knee, for the first time in a long while, I felt like asking if I could keep it! And I was light on my feet, almost floating across the pavement, but frustratingly I was barely catching him.

"Have we got long left dad?" I called.

"It's that thief again, son! He's at it again nicking it from right under our noses."

The sharpness to the buildings was going, it was like I was losing focus. I closed my eyes and shook my head hoping to clear my eyesight. When I opened them, dad was beginning to blur a little, too.

"You know I loved ... love you dad, don't you?" he looked back, then turned, his body softening and evaporating ever so slightly with the twirl.

"It's funny, but when your love is strong, yours, mums and Alan's ... it's like you all charge my batteries." he thumped his heavy chest. "So at the moment I'm running on Duracell's ... I am strong, burning bright, so keep me in your heart." he said, his voice a little quieter.

"Forever dad, I promise." I said with feeling, "The Lakes, dad, Windermere, was it okay to scatter your ashes there?"

"Absolutely perfect, Alan chose well. Each day I look out across beautiful scenery and feel alive again!"

"Mum was worried..."

"Tell her there is nothing she could of done when I passed and nothing she should feel bad about if she laughs ... tell her to make the most of the family's love, and tell her laugh lots ... think of me and feel happy, not sad."

"Before you go, dad, what happens to the...erm...naughty boys?" I looked and nodded downwards, hinting at a hotter place with furnaces.

"No, you can tell Stew he'll be fine ... he may spend a few years say sorry to all the people he has been a little bit horrible to ... so after a couple of decades he will be able to enjoy the same things all us good boys do!" He laughed again, but it was as if I was listening on a bad telephone line now. "But tell him to stop smoking ... he really is an empty head, isn't he?"

"Oh yeah ... once a numbskull." I agreed.

"Right Bri, I've just left Alan at the penguins. He's following them swimming around under water, watching them through the glass." dad started to melt away quicker now."...that ice cream ... it's all over his hands, but he's so happy ... are you?"

"Happier ... a lot better for being in Boggart Hole Clough with my hero. My chance to say thank you, for being my dad."

"Hero? Me? If only I was." he was just eyes and a mouth now ... everything else had dissolved ... but both were smiling. His voice ever more distant and feeble. "Bri, tell your mum I love her ... I love you and I love Alan ... I love all the family, thank them all for the past fifty odd years. God I was so..so..so..lucky. You know what, Bri? I loved it all ... every bloody second..." he had now disappeared ... become a mist, hanging just above me. A small breath of air started to carry him away. I reached up and my hand passed right through, causing swirls in the smoke. Then as I watched, my hand grew, hairs growing on the back of it, fingers stretching, veins coming into view, my true age becoming apparent ... boy to man ... I stretched and this time I woke, and I woke alone. I stared up at the ceiling, bright, warm sunshine was breaking through the gap between the curtains and hit the headboard to my right. It was time to get up ... time to give my life another go.

Printed in Great Britain
by Amazon